GETTING OFF

By Z

Skye Publishing

Skye Publishing Co.

P.O. Box 4562

Annapolis, MD 21403

Printed in the United States of America

First Printing: January 2007

Library of Congress Cataloging - in Publication Data:

ISBN # 0-9675160-3-X

One in every three people

in the United States

is a victim of a crime.

THE EVENTS AND CHARACTERS IN THIS BOOK ARE FACTUAL. HOWEVER, CERTAIN NAMES HAVE BEEN ALTERED IN ORDER TO PROTECT THE IDENTITY OF WITNESSES.

GETTING OFF

Table of Contents

Skye Publishing Co.

Taking you to
The Outer Limits.

FORWARD

GETTING OFF is the true saga of a woman's life as it unfolds during the end of World War II. This dark, but sometimes humorous account, takes the reader through a series of compelling dramas, including a bout with Polio, an attempted suicide, a failed marriage, her involvement with cryogenic suspension, and then at last, a successful career in advertising.

But then, at the height of her achievement she is brutally knifed in the presence of her 8 year old daughter. After more than a year passes, the alleged perpetrator is caught and the women, who we come to know by the name of "Z", is asked to be the star witness for the Prosecutor. As the case goes to trial, Z is confident that her assailant will be convicted and she will be free from the fear that had possessed her.

This work is dedicated
To Janet and Kenneth.

I. THE DEATH OF AN ANGEL

"We are the War Babies!"

The stark statement stunned the graduating class. The high school auditorium was suddenly quiet, the teenager's faces grim, their eyes staring at Harriet Kass, the class President.

That was a harsh beginning for a commencement program. She had meant to get our attention and she did. I found myself recalling vague memories of the end of the war...I couldn't have been more than twenty-two months old at the time.

I had on brown leather up-to-the ankle baby shoes. I remember them because I thought that they were ugly, and a dress that had blue flowers on it. I liked the little blue flower pattern, but the dress was itchy on my fair skin. My mother was rushing us into the damp, grey basement. The lights were out in the house and they were out on the street. Sirens had blared and it meant that there was an air raid. I was terrified. I wasn't really sure what "war" was, but I knew that it killed people and we had to hide in the basement. I knew that the "Japs" were our enemy.

My father wasn't with us. He had gone to his post on top of the Colony House Hotel. He was in the Civil Defense and wore a white arm band with big red initials on it: CD. I felt good about that because those were also *my* initials. His job was to watch for enemy airplanes. We lived in Great Neck, Long Island.

I remember the ration stamps and how my father was able to bring home black market meat.

Then it was all over. My mother heard it on the radio and was calling my grandmother. I was confused because I thought there was always going to be a war, it didn't occur to me that "wars" ended. I thought that it was a way of life...and I wasn't even two years old yet.

And there was Harriet standing at the podium in her purple and gold hat and gown. She was small, maybe only 5'1" or so with short black hair. I mused how it seemed that short people seemed to compensate by being aggressive like she was. I was tall, maybe the tallest girl in the class—5' 9-1/2". I was always tall and I liked being tall except when it came to boys because most of them were shorter than me.

It was my turn. I walked up onto the stage and was presented with my diploma. It was no thrill for me—I was glad to get out of high school.

My mother had given me an ultimatum-either I go to college or I go to work. I decided on college because it seemed easier than trying to find a job. What would I do? I couldn't type and I didn't want to be a secretary. I didn't realize that the talents that I *did* have could be cultivated and used to earn money. I was a good artist, musician and writer.

After I was born at Flushing Hospital on L.I. in New York (my daughter has a hard time believing that there is really a city called "Flushing")—my mother became very ill. She had contracted polio in the hospital. I spent the first few years of my life being cared for by nurses and relatives. I became an artist by the time I was two years old. I could spend hours entertaining myself by drawing and that included drawing all over the walls of my room.

We lived on the North Shore of the island in an upper-middle class three bedroom brick house. The house had oak floors and a master bedroom with a balcony, it was situated on a cul de sac. But it wasn't as wonderful as it appeared. My father was a hard-driven executive. His parents were Czechoslovakian immigrants who came to the U.S. when they were teenagers. As I recall the lore, they came here by boat, alone, unchaperoned, and settled in New York City in a Czech neighborhood on the upper east side. When they came of age, they married. My grandfather, who was a metal designer, got a job as a welder and wound-up working on the art deco tower of the Chrysler Building in New York. They had three children—my father-Frank, and my two aunts—Anna and Lillie. My grandfather was able to earn enough money to build a four-family house in Queens.

While he was working on the exterior of the Chrysler Building, on the tower—during the winter months, he contracted pneumonia. He died when he was about 30 or 31. My father who was the youngest of three kids, was 13 when his father passed away. I still remember a photo of my grandfather's face—his dark hair, his moustache and pale eyes.

Apparently my grandmother got some kind of compensation from Chrysler or the Metal Worker's Union because she never had to go to work. The house was paid for and there were always tenants in the other three apartments until my Aunt Anna got married. She married Julius Trinidad who was from Spain. My Uncle Julius was a very gentle man and all the kids loved him. Aunt Anna and Uncle Julius had three kids and took the apartment next to Grandma's in the four family house. Their kids (my cousins) were Nancy, Marion and Peggy. I lived in these two connecting apartments for a short while when my mother had polio. I was about 3 years old. Uncle Julius stayed home because he was sick and Aunt Anna worked in the city as a secretary. When I was about 7 or 8 years old Uncle Julius died of tuberculosis. I was very, very sad, because I liked him a lot, he was a loving and gentle man.

I went home from my paternal grandmother's house just before I was four. My mother was getting better. She could now get out of bed and walk but she had to wear special shoes with a "lift" in one of them because one leg was shorter than the other. Eventually (miraculously) the legs evened out and she could wear regular shoes.

At age four I was sent off to Buckley Country Day School in King's

Point. This was a private nursery school and some of my friends there were Shelly Caesar—Sid Caesar's daughter, and Ester Heifitz, Josha's daughter. I spent a year at Buckley and I distinctly remember two things: at nap time we slept on mattresses on the floor and during the year we produced a play—"Peter Pan". I was in the play but I have no recollection of what role I played. I know that I wasn't Tinkerbell because I desperately wanted that part but didn't get it.

So far my life seemed pretty grim. I came out of the war into a world of death and disease: tuberculosis, polio, pneumonia. By the time I entered Kindergarten I had also been hospitalized with bronchial pneumonia. But I was strong and I bounded back and made it all the way to the fourth grade with a spattering of things ranging from Chicken Pox and Measles to Tonsillitis and chronic nosebleeds.

Than at age 9, after spending two weeks away from home during the summer, at Brownie Camp, I, too, contracted polio.

At first my mother and the family doctor tried to treat me at home with bed rest and hot baths. But it was useless. My legs were paralyzed and I could see the fear in my mother's eyes. Finally one day my mother said that she had to cut off my hair; I had long blonde hair that I loved to play with. I could make all kinds of braided designs with my tresses and I was quite good at it. My mother said she had to cut it because I was bed-ridden and it was too hard for her to take care of.

The next night when my father got home from work, he came up to my room after dinner and carried me downstairs and put me into the back seat of our mauve-colored 1954 Hudson. My mother had made a bed in the back seat with a blanket and pillow. It was dark out. It was the end of August so it must have been around 8 pm. My mother said that we were going for a long drive to see a doctor.

I fell asleep in the back seat. When they woke me up we were at a big building. Two people were standing by the car. They were in white uniforms with blue headdresses. They opened the door and lifted me into a wheelchair. I was getting scared. I didn't know what was going on. They took me into the building along with my mother and father. Then my parents met privately with a doctor while I waited in the hallway in a wheelchair. After some time I was pushed into a room made of cinder blocks that had been painted white and had a green linoleum floor.

The doctor asked me some questions and then asked me to get out of the chair and walk. I struggled to get up on my feet and then a nurse helped me. I took a few steps. I felt very weak and it seemed that I had walked for miles. Finally they helped me back into the wheel chair and pushed me back out into the dreary hallway. I had thought that I walked pretty good. I had mustered all of my strength and forced myself to look as strong as possible because I thought that if I didn't walk good, they would make me stay there.

Well, apparently I didn't walk too good. Years later my mother told me that I had a bad limp and had only been able to take two dragging-type steps. To me, it seemed as though I had walked the full length of the room and back.

When they told me that I had to stay at the hospital, I cried uncontrollably. It must have been hard for my parents to leave. They had a long drive home.

I was so scared. I was put into a bed in a little hallway. There were 3 or 4 other kids there on beds. We were all waiting to get into the polio ward, but it was filled to capacity. I was in the Sister Kenny Institute. "There's nothing to be afraid of..." I heard a soft weak voice say. I turned my head. It was the girl on the bed next to me. "No one's going to hurt you here. My name is Clarissa" She barely spoke in a whisper. After a while I stopped crying and asked Clarissa a lot of questions. She looked thin and pale. Her body was completely paralyzed, and yet she seemed more concerned with me than her own fate. To me, she was like an angel, a fragile, sweet angel. I learned that she was 13 and she seemed to be very, very sick. Finally we slept.

I was awakened by nurses running by and yelling things. I was scared. I looked around and could see where they were going ... into a glass enclosed room with a large metal machine that looked like a huge tin can. The machine was making horrible sucking noises and I could see a child's head sticking out. I was terrified. Clarissa woke-up and explained to me that the menacing gray sputtering machine was an "iron lung". "It's to help that little girl to breathe." I thought that I'd be the next kid to go into the machine, but I didn't tell Clarissa. I just cried and cried. Suddenly it was very quiet and the machine was turned off. "She's gone ..." the nurse was saying. I *knew* what that meant. I knew that the little girl had died. And that's when I was sure that I was going to die, too.

The next day I was put into the children's ward. I was in a bed next to Doris. I wanted to know where my friend, Clarissa, was. No one would tell me. Late that afternoon, my mother came to the hospital. She came there every day for 10 months, traveling more than 130 miles each way to reassure me, to sneak vitamins to me, and to oversee my treatment.

During the first few months it was a grueling routine of hot pack treatments made from wool blankets and exercises. I worked with a therapist who, like the nurses, wore a sort of nun's headdress. Her gray dress was covered with a white apron. I wish I could remember her name. She was there every day. Her constant encouragement saved hundreds of children's lives.

Then I became 10 years old. By this time I had been in the Institute for one month. After a very serious setback where I had to be isolated because the polio virus had gone into my lungs, I was put back into the ward with Doris. It was that afternoon when I found out about Clarissa. I often asked about her, where she was ... they said she was with the older kids in another ward. But the truth was Clarissa had died. That was nearly 50 years ago, but I will never forget that sweet, sweet girl who got me through that frightening first night at the Sister Kenny Institute. Somewhere out there, there is an angel named Clarissa.

I got progressively better. I was in a wheel chair, and on my free afternoons, after therapy and time with my school tutor, I would whizz down to the baby ward at the end of the hall. The large room was filled with small cribs lined-up side by side. I would sit by the babies in my wheel chair and sing lullabies to them until I had to go back to my ward. And everyday my mother would bring me vitamins and I would take them on her cue when no one was looking because my mother was told that she wasn't allowed to give me anything like that. But I trusted and believed my mother and took the vitamins.

Finally, just after Easter, I got the news. I was going home! Home! I was so happy. I was walking. I had been at the Institute for nearly ten months. When my parents escorted me out of the hospital, there were photographers outside from the *N.Y Herald Tribune*. They were talking to my parents and with two doctors and calling me a "miracle case". Apparently, the prognosis was that I would never walk again; but there I was—walking down the stone steps at the front of the Institute. I didn't really understand how lucky I was. I didn't yet understand the courage and brevity that I had learned—not yet.

After three years of physical therapy, I was given a clean bill of health. I was a polio survivor with no pronounced disabilities. I was 13.

Why I started smoking at age 13-1/2 is beyond me. I guess it was to look grown-up. It was part of the persona that I was acquiring: eye make-up, blush, lipstick and nail polish.; an avid obsession with boys. Suddenly, boys were everywhere. Where did they come from? They were never around before. There were always the neighborhood boys that I grew up with—Johnny, Fuzzy, Michael, Henry and Walrus. But they were different—they were like my brothers. I was in junior high and boys and girls were going to dances and holding hands and necking in the movies.

I didn't have a real boyfriend until I was 15. We met during the first term of my sophomore year at Great Neck South. He was new in town. I had gotten off the bus near the candy store which was an after-school hang-out. He walked right up to me. His hair wasn't dark blonde and it wasn't gray—it was taupe and it was what we called "kinky"—tight waves. This gangling teen had green eyes, a hooked nose and sensuously curved lips. He was about an inch shorter than me. Larry was a Jew. I was not. But I never really thought about it one way or another. He lived in the apartment complex just down the hill from my parents' home. We were told that people in the garden apartments were sort of low-income. Most of my high-school friends lived there—the two Andys, Pam; who was half Chinese and half Indian, Pat—who was my brother's girlfriend until he started beating her up, Hal—until he committed suicide because he was gay, Niti—whose mother sang at the little local night club, and Bret and Dotty—a red haired bespeckled mother with a retarded son. There were at least ten other kids that I knew there, but Larry and Andy were my best friends until one day, in the dingy apartment hallway, Larry kissed me. Then he was my boyfriend.

At first, I liked Larry because he played the piano and he laughed a lot, and then that friendship evolved into one of passion and deep emotion. Can a 15 year-old experience that? Most definitely. We weren't rebellious or delinquent types. I had a curfew, did my homework, helped around the house and pursued my interest in art and music. Larry got a job after school as a soda jerk at the candy store. Larry and I always went out Friday and Saturday nights. We'd go to the movies, to the Italian restaurant or to school affairs. In school, we started the Library Club together. And then there were the times when we'd sneak up to the roof of his building to make-out; or down in the basement hallways. There weren't a lot of places we could go. It was a wonderful relationship. Particularly since we both loved classical music. He taught me to play Für Elise on the piano. We just loved being together, alone, and with our crowd of friends. We weren't always goody-two-shoes, either. Once, Andy, Larry and me stole Dotty's car. We knew where she left the keys in the car, so one afternoon we took it for a spin. I was the driver. I was terrified that I'd end-up in jail. I only drove it about three blocks, turned around and took the car back to the garage. Only the three of us knew and we never did it again. We were 15. We were just kids having a good time.

Then one day in June, almost at the end of the school year, my mother suddenly told me that I couldn't go out with Larry any more. I was devastated and confused. There was no reason, in my mind, that we shouldn't be allowed to be together. I felt like we were Romeo & Juliet. My mother told me that she had called Larry's mother and told her that he had to stay away from me. Why? I begged and pleaded. I hated my mother for that. I just hated her. I spent most of the summer depressed and withdrawn. Larry never called me after that and we avoided each other in school for the next two years. So, why did she break it up? Because he was Jewish.

I had gone to Temple with Larry several times and enjoyed the services. They were different from my Protestant upbringing; more ceremonial and in Hebrew that I couldn't understand. My mother never knew that I had attended those services, and I did not understand why I couldn't date a Jew, after all, Great Neck was about 90% Jewish.

It took me a long time to get over what my mother had done. I went to the Junior Prom the following year with some friends. Larry was there, but we didn't speak to each other. I had long since dropped out of our Library Club and spent my junior and senior years with other friends—mostly June and Angela.

For the Senior Prom, I invited John, a good-looking, sharp, tall Italian kid who was fairly new in town. It was rumored that his father was in the mob. My girlfriend, June, was madly in love with John's older brother, Angelo. Sometimes we'd go over to John's house after school and the four of us would slow-dance in his basement. John was a fabulous dancer. His family had moved to Great Neck from Brooklyn the year before. His father was in the "construction" business. That business must have paid pretty good because they lived in a stunning house and had a Cadillac. In those days, if you had a Cadillac, you were very rich. I asked John to the Senior Prom because he was a Junior and he couldn't ask me. He said yes, and I was thrilled. I had a crush on John but it was meaningless to me because he was a no-brainer. I think I asked him to the prom to get back at Larry; to show him up. Even though it wasn't Larry's fault that we broke up, I blamed him anyway; maybe because he wasn't chivalrous. Larry went to the Prom with a female friend of his who wasn't very impressive. At least I had a great time. John really knew how to dance, he was like a John Travolta, same look, same Brooklyn accent, same dance moves. He got to use his father's Cadillac for the Prom, too. After the Prom we doubled with Andy and his date and drove into the City. John's father had fixed it up so that we could go to the Copa. It was an unbelievable experience.

The Copacabana was the hottest spot in New York then (as Barry Manilow will attest) and here we were—a group of seventeen year olds, sitting at the best table in the house, watching the fabulous entertainment, and having real cocktails. At that point I was convinced that John's father worked for the Mafia, and I thought that was kind of groovy. We left the Copa around 3 a.m. Most of the kids would drive out to the beach, as was customary, but John didn't offer to take me—he just drove me home. He didn't even kiss me goodnight. I could never figure that one out. We never went out after that.

Right after graduation, my mother gave me an ultimatum: College or go get a job. I was late to apply for college. It was approaching July when I got all the applications out. My mother did most of the work, but she was going after schools that were out of town—mostly in Boston. I wasn't happy about it but I didn't have much choice. Towards the end of July, while I was waiting for responses from the schools, I was invited by a male friend to a baseball game. It was about a month before my 18th birthday. It had been a boring summer so far, so I went to the game. There, I found myself unable to take my eyes off of one of the pitchers. I didn't know a lot about baseball, but this guy was good. After the game we were all going to the beach for a party; the team and a lot of the spectators. It was a night party. We had a bonfire and made hotdogs. Beer was flowing as uncontrollably as the ocean. I didn't like the stuff, but I drank it anyway. It gave me enough nerve to go after that cute pitcher. I wound up making out with him on the beach and then we both were rolling in laughter when the guys stripped Bob Leary naked and wouldn't give him back his clothes. I liked this group—they were fun!

It turned out that most of *that* crowd had gone to Great Neck North (the *other* high school). If you went to GN North you were either very rich and from the King's Point area, or you were Catholic.

The baseball team was mostly Catholic kids and Tim, the pitcher, became my new boyfriend. He was 19 and was home on leave from the Navy. He was stationed at Newport, R.I. When he went back to his base we started up a pen-pal relationship which lasted almost 2 years. When I realized the proximity of Boston to Newport, I was glad that I was going to be attending school there. I had been accepted at Chamber-layne Junior College; a division of Boston University. It was right on Commonwealth Avenue by the Charles River.

II. GOING OVERBOARD

My father took the train with me when I first entered the school. He helped me with all of my luggage and got me settled into the dorm. I was put way up on the third floor in a tiny room by myself because I requested no roommates.

Well, I quickly met a lot of girls (in those days there were no co-ed dorms) and within a week I moved downstairs to share a room with Saundra and "Bing". I also became friends with Gloria and Judy who were also from L.I., Saundra was from Haverhill, Mass., and Bing was from Connecticut. Bing was a total nut. She was sort of a tomboy and very big. She was as tall as me, but probably weighed about 250 lbs. Saundra and I argued with her constantly because she wanted to keep the windows wide open at night when it was only 20° outside, and it wasn't just the chill—it was also our fear of the Boston strangler, he was still lurking on the streets and some of his victims hadn't been so far away.

I loved my classes. I was studying art and architecture with a minor in English prose. This was nothing like high school—it was *really* interesting, and Timmie came up to Boston every 3 or 4 weeks. He was always in his sailor's uniform and all the girls thought he was really cute.

In November, he got a week off for Thanksgiving and so we took a Greyhound bus home together. It was the Fall of 1962 and in those days, you could smoke on the bus. Hell! You could smoke on the train, on the planes, on a boat, in the movies, in the grocery store; you could smoke wherever the hell you wanted to!

We were smoking virgins. By then, I was 18 and Timmie was 20. We did everything but the "deed". Timmie—being an Irish Catholic, respected my virginity. But when I went home for Thanksgiving, my friend, June, told me she had done "it" with Angelo. She sort of implied that it was o.k. to do "it" after you were 18. After all, in New York, when you were 18, you could drink alcohol and vote.

While we were home for the holidays, we went to a party at June's house. Her parents were away. It was pretty much a drinking party. She had a nice rec room with a ping pong table and a bar. I loved to play ping pong.

During the party, with June's encouragement, Timmie and I took off to one of the bedrooms for a make-out session. Our session had plenty of body-part fondling and I finally said, "Let's do it!". He said, "Are you sure?" I was sure. I was ready and so was he. Well, it took about 38 seconds ... It was the old joke about the Irish penis—"Is it in?" I was disappointed and a bit frustrated by his premature ejaculation, but after all—he was a 20 year old virgin. He had told me that he didn't even jerk-off because of his Catholic upbringing.

After that, sex became an integral part of our relationship. It also became a nightmare because we were too stupid to think about birth control, and though, after that first time, our sessions began to last a bit longer than 38 seconds, I was lucky not to have gotten pregnant. I *did* start taking birth control pills after Christmas, and that alleviated most of our fears.

In January I started a part-time job a few days a week after school. I was doing really great, getting straight A's on my report card. It was my first "real" job. I was a telephone solicitor for the Johns-Manville Corp., selling aluminum siding. I liked the job, and I liked my boss. He was a young Greek guy named Dean. He was maybe in his late 20's and married. He was the manager. This tall, olive-skinned dark-haired smooth-talker was very attractive to me, and I found myself working pretty hard for him. I wanted his approval, I guess.

In the beginning of February, my roommate Saundra told me that she was pregnant. She had decided to drop-out of school and marry her childhood sweetheart, Stan. Bing was also moving out because she was a non-smoker and wanted her wide-open windows. I had become friends with a gal in the dorm who we called "Corky". I have no idea where that came from. She was from a rich family in Dallas, TX, and along with her Southern drawl, she was a bourbon-drinking, cussing, red-haired hussie. She was fun, so I asked her to move in with me since I had no roommates.

One day, Dean asked me if I wanted to go have a drink with him after work. Since #1-he was my boss, and #2-I had a crush on him, I accepted. We had fun. We went to an Irish Pub near my dormitory. During the evening he asked me if me and my roommate might like to hook-up with him and his friend, Steve, some night. I didn't ask him about his situation with his wife. I was pretty naive about things like that, and, although I was "going" with Timmie, I figured, what's the big deal?

When I got back to the dorm, I asked Corky if she wanted to double on a blind date and of course she said yes. I had heard things about Corky in the dorm, that she was pretty loose, but that didn't phase me.

So we met Dean and Steve for drinks about a week later. I wasn't much of a drinker, so when it was pretty late and everyone was feeling no pain, someone was talking about going to a motel. I didn't know what the hell was going on, so I said o.k. and Corky was all for it. The next thing I knew, Corky and Steve were on a bed screwing and Dean and I were on the other bed trying to screw, but it wasn't happening. It wasn't happening because I was used to my "Is it in?" Irishman, and Dean had an enormous piece of Greek equipment that just would not fit into my garage. Dean rolled off of me and I think he quickly realized that I was not terribly experienced. When we got back to the dorm, Corky and I didn't talk about it much. I don't think that she knew that my session with Dean was unsuccessful, but still, I felt terribly guilty. I had cheated on Timmie. I knew that he would have never done that to me, and I never told him about it.

That Winter and early Spring just flew by. After my encounter with Dean, I never went back to work. I just didn't show up and he never called me. It was probably a case of mutual embarrassment. I missed the extra money, but I really needed the time to study and to write letters to Timmie. I also did my share of partying. After all, that was Boston and there were frat parties everywhere. I met a lot of great guys too, but I never dated any of them. I remained true to Timmie.

Towards the end of April, Timmie invited me down to Newport, to the Navy Base. His ship, the U.S.S. J.P. Kennedy, was having an open house. I had been to Newport once before. Timmie and me had shacked-up at the "Base Motel". I remember it distinctly, because after we had made love, I said, "C'mon! Let's take a shower together!" Well, he found that to be offensive, somehow, something to do with his Catholic upbringing.

The Open House on the ship sounded like fun. I asked Corky if she wanted to go too, because she had been dating Timmie's ship-mate, "Red". Corky was a party-girl and of course she said yes.

I actually forged a permission slip to go away for the weekend and gave it to the Dorm Mother. Corky didn't need one because her parents had given her carte blanche permission to do whatever the hell she wanted to.

We left Saturday morning and took the bus down to Newport. We checked into separate rooms at the Base Motel. Then we took a cab over to the Base and met Tim and Red on the destroyer. It was a pretty ritzy gathering because this was the Destroyer named after the President's brother, the one that President Kennedy, Jacqueline, Caroline and John-John went on to watch the infamous yacht race between the Weatherly and the Gretel the previous year; and it was the ship that went to Cuba during the crisis, and on October 26, 1962, the Kennedy team boarded the SS Marucla, a Lebanese ship that had been leased by Russia and was looming in Guantanamo Bay as a threat against the United States.

So this "Open House" was a celebration of sorts, of the ships successful mission to Cuba seven months prior, during a very critical period in history. Timmie had been on that mission and had later written to me about how scary it really was. In fact, he said, that's when he decided that he would complete his 2 years in the Navy and then get the hell out!

I had dressed up to go on board. I was wearing a black Polka-dotted silk blouse with a black skirt and the only pair of black leather Papagallo's (shoes) that I owned.

Shortly after boarding, the next thing I remember was the shocking bite of the freezing water. I was fighting my way to the top of the water while choking and gasping for air. I had fallen overboard. I had been leaning on the life line and talking to someone when suddenly the life line gave way and there I was—beneath the water. I don't even remember hitting the side of the ship docked in the next berth. I was pretty hysterical and in a complete state of shock. I was unconscious when I went into the frigid water and somehow—probably from the impact with the water—I regained consciousness. I was screaming and fighting to stay above the frigid water. This would be my second flirtation with death, my second lesson about courage and brevity.

The accident created complete chaos on the ship. It was a miracle that I hadn't drowned. As it turned out, a sailor was lowered down to me and he put me in a life preserver and I was hoisted up to the deck of the ship.

Once on board I was taken to sick bay. Corky went with me. There they asked me to remove my drenched clothes and they gave me some sort of robe to put on. While they took my clothes to be dried, I was asked to lie down—but I couldn't, I was in so much pain—it was agonizing. Then they gave me a shot of brandy or whisky. My limbs were blue.

Later I was taken by an ambulance to the Base Hospital for x-rays and a thorough exam. Again, Corky went with me.

Hours later, Corky and me were taken to the Base Motel and the following day we were driven back to Boston.

Years later, I wrote a book about the episode. My parents wound-up suing the U.S. Government for negligence. We won and settled out of court. And again, I survived all odds.

My life was amassing many esoteric events. Yeah, I was sure a War Baby!

When I got back to school I was in sheer agony.

"Jesus Christ! What an experience!" Corky drawled.

I thought that she was acting peculiar. She seemed nervous and she smoked a lot. She didn't say much while we unpacked. "You want me to help you unpack?" she asked me. "No, I'll be o.k. You know, after the accident all I could think of when they were pulling me up in the life preserver was whether they could see up my skirt" Corky laughed, "Christ! At a moment like that—who'd care?" "Yeah, you're right, but I was still embarrassed." Corky shrugged. "I'm going over to the Greek's for a beer. Ya'll wanna come?" she asked. "No, my back really hurts. I"m going to lie down for awhile. But would you bring me back a pack of Marlboro's?" "Sure will".

When she came back a few hours later she was feeling no pain. She obviously had more than just a "few" beers. She flopped onto her bed.

"What a mess! What a goddam mess!" "What are you talking about, Corky?"

"I never got to see Red while we were in Newport. I stood him up. I was supposed to meet him for dinner Saturday night." "Why didn't you? I thought you went out with him after they brought me back to the Motel." Corky didn't answer. Suddenly she was crying. Not hysterically, just sort of whimpering like a puppy. "Corky?" "I don't want to talk about it." "Corky!—What happened? Isn't it bad enough that I fell off the ship and almost died?" "Jesus, I don't know what to do..." "To *do*? To do about what? About Red? Why didn't you meet him?" Then she blurted: "Because he raped me! That goddam son-of-a-bitch asking the questions, the Naval Officer asking the questions about you falling off the ship raped me! He invited me out to dinner to interrogate me and then took me back to my room at the Base Motel and he raped me!"

"Oh, my God! Oh God, Corky, no."

"Corky, you've got to report this to the police!" "I can't." "Why not?"

They were having dinner at a seafood restaurant near the naval base. The investigator asked Corky what she would like to drink. "Why, I'm Southern, you know, so I'll have a bourbon and water." "Well, I'll be ... that's my favorite ..." replied the Officer.

After several rounds of drinks, the two ordered dinner. It wasn't until a little after eleven o'clock, when they left the restaurant. He drove her back to the Base Motel. "Would ya like a night cap?" Corky inquired. "Sure!" He came into the room. She poured two glasses of bourbon.

"So you didn't really see your roommate go overboard, did you?"

"Yes, I did." He moved closer to her. "I don't think you understand what I'm saying. You did *not* see her fall off the ship. "But I did!" He grabbed her by the arm. "Let me go!"

"Let me tell you something, lady, I'm a Federal Officer, and you'll do what I tell you to. And if you say anything against me, I'll tell them that you're a goddam whore."

He reached into his pants pocket and pulled out a twenty dollar bill and threw it in her face. Corky was speechless. She felt trapped and helpless. He was blackmailing her and she couldn't do anything about it. She was afraid to scream or fight him off. He was armed with a gun. She decided to just play along with it until she could get him to leave.

"Take your clothes off, bitch..."

Eventually it was over. Before he left her room he said, "Just remember, Kiddo, if you say anything to anybody about this, I'll get you into the slammer for hooking." He turned around and shut the door. It was about 2 a.m.

"Don't you see, he has me trapped. I can't talk about this and you can't either ... ever. Promise me you won't."

In 1963 there were no rape crisis centers where Corky could go. For a few days she just hung around the dorm and sulked. It was mid-May and there were only a few weeks of school left. Neither of us ever went back to our classes. Corky returned to Texas, never to be heard from again. Me? I went home early, too. My father came up to Boston to get me and help me with all of my luggage. I could still barely walk and my back felt like an over-used trampoline. We flew home from Boston in a prop plane. I had never flown before and I was terrified. My father jokingly said, "We should have taken the plane that has the windshield wipers on the inside." I was as green as moldy white bread when I got off the plane.

I spent that summer recuperating from this horrendous accident. And because my parents were suing the U.S. government for negligence, I couldn't even talk about it. My mother said right then and there that I was staying home and should consider continuing my college education in New York City ... specifically at Parsons School of Design.

I didn't care. I was depressed and in a lot of pain. Timmie came home on leave as often as he could but things weren't the same. He didn't seem to care much that I was still in agony.

In August I got a job in a local boutique putting back clothes that were left in the try-on rooms but that only lasted two weeks. My back had not recovered enough for me to stand for long periods of time. It was like having Polio all over again.

I got accepted at Parson's. It was a short commute to N.Y.C. from where we lived on Long Island. By September I was feeling a lot better and was eager to start school. I was majoring in Fine Art with courses in design, printing, English prose and a minor in Psychology. Parsons was a division of N.Y.U. at that time. It was located on the East Side in the posh 50's (Fifty-Fourth Street). On my first day of class, I met Boyd. He was a tall blue-eyed blonde, very Scandinavian looking with a squared jaw. He was a talented artist.

There were only a handful of boys in my classes. Most of them were gay or of questionable sexuality. I became friends with Susan, a very Jewish-type of girl from Brooklyn. Very Jewish brought to mind Barbara Streisand—she was very Barbara Striesandish: motherly; aggressive, and blatantly frank. That rawness appealed to me. Adrianne was more reserved. Her life at home must have been pallidly prim because she painfully forced herself into a pose of superiority and self-righteousness. "I'm from Forest Hills." was about all she would say about herself but she made it a cloying fact that she was a very rich Forest Hills person. JoAnne was from the Bronx. Very hip, very arty, and very stoned. Her long thick brown hair appeared to have been crushed and slept on, her blue eyes bleary, her speech thick with Brooklynese and booze. The three of us wound-up being a clan at school. On Fridays we'd go to the New York deli around the corner for lunch. It was the only day we really got together and I always ordered the same thing: a runny Western omelette and a baked potato with tons of coffee. Coffee had become an integral part of my life. I had a grueling schedule, starting at 6 a.m. and often not getting to bed until after midnight. But, I really loved those days...1963...New York City...art movements...President Kennedy...the beginning of the Vietnam War...Andy Warhol...it was dynamic environment.

III. SUICIDAL HIGH

Boyd walked up to me and introduced himself. He was very charming, handsome, straight, very concentrated. He was from Freehold, New Jersey. Oddly, his family lived in a trailer. Oddly, because I never knew or even could fathom someone living in a trailer. While at Parson's, he was living in an apartment in Queens in an area which was mostly Indian, Persian and Pakistani. He had two roommates, both students—Richard (Dick), an American studying Architecture at Parsons, and "Allie", a Persian studying dentistry at N.Y.U.

Boyd and me rapidly became tied at the hip friends. He asked me on day one about my romantic status. I told him that I was going with Timmie; that he was away in Newport-in the Navy. I didn't tell him about my accident on the destroyer. I never really figured it out, but I think Boyd liked to face a challenge such as luring me away from Timmie. He was good. Within two weeks he was kissing me in the elevator at school, and two weeks later we were making love in his apartment.

He never came out and said that he was a virgin; it was just a gut-feeling that I had, assisted by his angel-like demeanor. But when we made love that first time on his little cot in the corner of the dingy two-room apartment it was a revelation to me. He was gentle, romantic, erotic and sensuously verbal. Afterwards, he would spend a long time sketching portraits of me. Within a few weeks I was naively smitten...sucked into his egocentricity with gravitational force... blinded by his self-centered id...wet from his sexual appetite.

"When are you going to tell Timmie?" I hadn't considered that. I wasn't really ready to break-off my two-year relationship. Timmie and I had talked about marriage, about kids. He knew my family, and I knew his: his freckled Irish family of six kids with alcoholic parents. (Albeit, they were good parents). This relationship was too new, too consuming, too all-or-nothing. Timmie was away most of the time and on weekends Boyd went home to visit his parents and his sister at their trailer park.

Finally, early in October, he gave me an ultimatum ... "I can't be with you if I can't have you all to myself ..." We were already a "thing" at school. He was not shy about being openly affectionate with me in class, and it made me the envy of all of the girls—particularly Anne. Anne was a small, thin, pale blonde with straight hair down to her waist. She was older than most of us ... maybe 25 or 26. She had already studied at the Art Student's League and her paintings were bold statements of pastel planes, non-objective hard-edged muted mauves and gray. She was studying fine art. She was very good and as cold and calculating as her paintings.

She became chummy with Boyd. I avoided her. There was something artificially icy about her as well as an "I'm-older-than-you" superiority complex. My friends ignored her, too.

Late in October I invited Boyd out to Great Neck on a Friday night. I wanted him to meet my parents and my friends. Fridays had become McDonnell's night: the night all the local college kids went to the bar to drink beer and have philosophical chats about existentialism, the looming war in Vietnam, and share academic experiences. So I introduced him to my parents and my mother let me borrow her car to take him to the bar.

The place was packed and reeked of booze and smoke. Kids were shooting pool in the back room. A few of my friends were already seated in one of the booths— Pat (my brother's ex-girlfriend), and Nanci. We joined them. I thought we were all having a great time; telling jokes, gossiping and laughing. After a couple of drinks I excused myself to go to the ladies' room. While in there I had a few sad thoughts about Timmie. I had finally told him about Boyd a couple of weeks before and he was devastated. I had prayed that I had done the right thing. My relationship with Boyd was magic—he was the magician, I was the lady in the box getting sawed in half. The professors at school gave us knowing looks, especially Marvin Israel and Mr. Sokol. They were my two favorite teachers and obviously they were getting a big rip over our flaming relationship.

I went back out to the booth. Boyd was gone. The girls told me that he went to the men's room. After a long while he hadn't returned. Suddenly I had a queasy premonition that something was awfully wrong. I went over to the bar and asked one of the guys to look in the men's room...no one there. I looked everywhere in the bar. He was definitely gone. I drove to the train station, not there, I drove around town for an hour looking for him. I was stunned. What the hell?

Finally, I went home. I didn't tell my mother what happened. On Saturday I tried calling him at the apartment. Dick said that he had been there but left in the morning to go to New Jersey.

Ohhh Kay. I'll just see what he says to me on Monday when I get back to class, I mused. Well, on Monday he avoided me like the plague and pretty much suckered up to Anne. I had no clue. I spent days trying to figure it out. Besides being devastated by the jilt, I was also insulted. He wasn't talking to me and I'd be damned if I was going to talk to him. And that was that.

I became very depressed by the whole incident. Susan and Adrianne were digging, trying to get something out of me—but I wasn't talking, I just said, flatly, "It's over, that's all."

I buried myself in school work, determined to outdo everyone...to make the Dean's List. In November I ran into Timmie at McDonnell's. It was a night when my parents were away and I was still feeling very low.

I wanted to go back with Timmie, but for selfish reasons; because of my bruised ego, because I needed someone. I sat down next to him at the bar and we small-talked and drank... It was awkward. Finally, I blurted it out: I told him how sorry I was, that I wanted him back. He said "no way, once burnt, blah, blah, blah." I told him that I was going to go home and take a bottle of sleeping pills if he didn't go back with me. He laughed. So I did. I went home and swallowed about 20 of my mother's phenobarbital. Then I drove back to McDonnell's. I stumbled up to the bar and pretty much told anyone who would listen that I had OD'd on sleeping pills, that I was committing suicide because of my split with Timmie. At first, Joey, the bartender/owner thought I was being melodramatic. Timmie was there and was becoming embarrassed. I was drinking a rye and soda...mumbling and bleary-eyed from the narcotic.

As with all of my near-death experiences, there was redemption. In this case, McDonnell's was located next door to the Fire House. Instinct and experience told Joey to get an ambulance after I passed out.

All I could remember is waking up in the hospital. I felt sick and groggy. Then my mother came in. She looked as bleary-eyed as I did. "Oh God, why'd you do it?" "Ma, it was stupid. It was because of Timmie, to get his attention." That's all I could say. She shook her head. She was utterly at a loss—she thought I was still going with Boyd. I had to stay in the mental ward for several days. During that time I met with the psychiatrist and I realized that in order to get out of this place, I had to convince him of my sanity; that it was simply a matter of unrequited love and nothing more.

According to the book, *Insanity Art and Culture* by Francis Rectman: The relationship between the artist and insanity is that "In some cases of schizophrenia there is a progressive disintegration of the personality, and the paintings of such patients reflect this." "Several of the descriptive definitions of schizophrenia are incomplete; one might as well be content with the description of it by the sixteenth century scholar, Rubert Burton, who says: “Most part they are afraid, they are bewitched, possessed, or poisoned by their neighbours, and sometimes they suspect their nearest friends...”

That was me alright, I was a bewitched and possessed artist who poisoned herself with phenobarbital.

After that I never saw Timmie again. In the Spring of ‘64, he got out of the Navy and moved to California. I spent the remainder of my year at Parsons buried in my studies and judiciously avoided Boyd and Anne, who were, by then, an item and living together.

In June, my report card reflected my earnestness and I received straight A’s. I still had two more years to go before I graduated and I used those two years to develop my skills as a fine artist and a graphic artist. I also worked on my persona and took my future very seriously.

The tedious work at school had its just rewards. In May, 1966, shortly before I was to graduate, I was offered a job by one of the Professors, Abe Greiss, who was the V.P. and Creative Director of Advertising at Macy’s. At that time there was only ONE Macy’s—1 Herald Square—New York—dubbed “The World’s Largest Store.” I was to start there after graduation.

My parents were extraordinarily proud of my achievements. I had gone from a so-so bumbling student in high school to a Dean’s List graduate at Parson’s School of Design.

The lawsuit against the U.S. Government was still in progress, a very, very slow progress. Although I still had lower back pain, I did not let it affect my performance. I spent two glorious years at Macy’s—first as a layout artist, and then I was an art director for five soft-goods departments until 1968.

That year I finally decided to take a break. I needed a vacation. For two years I had worked five days a week at Macy's with no vacation, so in August of '68, I decided to take a week off and vacation in San Juan, Puerto Rico. I hated flying. Thank God you could still smoke on the airlines then...even so, my knuckles were as white as my cigarettes and it was excruciating for me.

I loved the Island. My Spanish was good enough to talk with the locals and I met a lot of partying and perfunctionary people. Life was good there. It wasn't stressful like New York. I figured that since the Puerto Rican's were going to New York, I'd be a New Yorker going to Puerto Rico. When I got back from my vacation, I quit my job at Macy's and moved to San Juan, just like that. In two week's time, and within a week of my relocation, I found an apartment and a job there.

I had landed a position as a designer at an Ad Agency. It was one of the top agencies there handling accounts like the El Conquistador Hotel, Lancome Cosmetics, and Puerto Rican Independent Airlines—to name a few...and even better yet—I fell in love with my boss—Humberto. "Bert" was one of the agency's proprietors. He told me that he was 29. (I think that he was a little older than that). He was tall, dark and exceedingly handsome—always with a big grin on his square face; and he was rich. He had a slick steel and glass bachelor pad with white leather couches and a walk-in closet full of Armani suits. He also had a live-in valet who laid-out his clothes and maintained his condo. Bert was a member of the San Juan Yacht Club and, of course, had a yacht, which he dubbed the "Manta Ray".

For several months I was living the kind of soap opera you read about in *Cosmopolitan*...Young, hip, tall, green-eyed blonde with a dream job in advertising, having an affair with the boss. I didn't realize how shallow my values were at the time but I knew that I was in love with

Bert. We'd go out deep-sea fishing on his yacht and then come back to the club and hang around on the boat. Bert liked drinking with his deck hands who were locals and didn't speak English. He also sang and played the guitar. He was everything I ever dreamed of.

I was canned from the Agency in November. I'm not sure why. Bert didn't fire me—it was the senior partner. That night I called Bert. He wasn't at home. I went down to the yacht club and found him on his boat with the guys. I confronted him. He acted surprised that I had been fired and swore that he knew nothing about it or why. I never knew why either. I've always suspected it was because I was having an affair with Bert.

It was impossible to find another job. I had saved enough money to see me through a few weeks. Bert was avoiding me and I got the impression that it was over.

That was it. During the first week of December I went home. Stupidly, I told myself that it was just for the holidays, so I left a lot of my stuff in the apartment in Puerto Rico. I thought I could borrow some money from my father and go back after Christmas. Wrong. I stayed at my parents' house and my father's response was, "Get a job!" Well, what I wound-up getting was pneumonia. I was really sick. My mother had gone to Phoenix for the winter so I was there with my father who, of course, was at work all day. I spent weeks in bed. My father, who was a smoker, took my cigarettes away. I was very depressed. I spent a lot of that time writing morose prose...

> Am I to be lost, or to be aware
> That loss is soon to be here?
> An epic moment, I couldn't care,
> That moment to live I would fear.

Is it one who searches now
Finding no path, but stone?
A barren moment; an empty vow,
To see again.. I'm alone.

Am I wandering, was I to be free?
In wandering from time found rarely?
This is my moment before destiny
In which I shall prevail...but barely.

In February (it was now 1969) I was finally getting better and my strength was coming back. I also found out that since I had been fired in Puerto Rico (a Commonwealth), I could collect unemployment compensation. I started smoking again. I called Abe Griess to see if I could get my job back at Macy's. "You sure can—but we have no openings right now—but I'll let you know the minute that I do." The bad news was that I had left my portfolio in Puerto Rico and couldn't get a job elsewhere without it, so I waited for Abe's precious call.

I started going to McDonnell's on Friday nights. I had no car so I took the bus. One night a familiar face confronted me and remarked: "You're Dicky's sister!" I laughed. That was a hell of a way to start a conversation. Standing before me was a tall, good-looking cocky-sort-of-guy. He was a neighbor whom I had grown up with. We were never very good friends because I always thought he was kind of fresh to me—mean spirited, and also kind of snooty, but I always thought he was kind of cute. That night he was wearing jeans, black combat boots and a khaki Air Force jacket. I assumed he was protesting the war or something. "Hi, Richard.," I said flatly, not terribly interested. I was sort of hoping to see Timmie, but Richard persisted. He asked me about what I had been doing since high school. I told him a few things and then he told me that he had just returned from Vietnam. That was awesome. I wanted to hear all about *that*.

Suddenly it was around one a.m. in the morning. "You wanna go to the diner for breakfast?" he offered. "Sure." We got into his tiny British racing green 1958 MG and went to the Star Diner. That was the same car he had in high school seven years before.

It was all because I was on the rebound. I was still moping over Bert, my lack of a career; my lack of self-esteem, and my lack of a life. Richard was witty and gruff; he also was out of a career, he had finished his two year tour of duty in Danang and was glad to be honorably discharged from the Air Force. We were two of a kind: aloft, abashed and at odds.

We quickly evolved into passionate lover-buddies; joined at the hip hippies with no job, no precise plans and no responsibilities. He drank a lot. For two months we partied and had abandoned, wonton sex wherever we could, including in his parents' bathtub. We thought we were in love.

On April Fool's Day he announced that he had gotten a job in Albany, N.Y., at the little airport there, as a mechanic. "But I'll come back every weekend to see you. Some day, I'm going to marry you..."

Then all hell broke loose ... Abe Greiss called me to let me know that I could have my old job back at Macy's. And the attorney representing the Navy in regard to my parent's lawsuit called telling my mother that they were anxious to settle prior to the scheduled trial—we had already had the pre-trial hearings in March.

With this sudden gush of money looming before me, I made plans to return to Puerto Rico and retrieve my belongings that I had left there.

It was comfortable working at Macy's again; and by the end of

April we settled the lawsuit. We settled for a pittance. The Navy admitted their negligence and made an offer. My parents took it and gave me $10,000.00 for my pain and suffering. Good grief!

I was still seeing Richard on weekends, and in the beginning of May, I told him that I had to go to Puerto Rico for a few days. He wasn't happy about it, but offered to drive me to the airport and pick me up upon my return.

After I checked into the Howard Johnson's, I called Bert. I was staying at the HoJo's in San Juan because it was two blocks from Bert's condo. He sounded delighted to hear from me. I *knew* why I called him, I was still head over heels with him and *had* to see him. I had an appointment the next day with the apartment manager. She had put my things in storage after I didn't return. She said I owed her money—and I told her that was okay—I'd pay her, I just wanted my things back—especially my portfolio.

Bert opened the door and stood barefoot in his teal-blue shorts and t-shirt, grinning with what appeared to be delight with my unannounced return. He offered me some rum and we chatted for awhile. Then he began to play his guitar. I should have humbly enjoyed that, but no, I made a total ass out of myself and started saying how I was getting married and too bad for you, you had your chance. I went on and on. He had stopped playing the guitar and just sat there with his eyes closed. He didn't say anything—not one word. Finally, I just got up and left. That was the end of that. I don't know what was the matter with me. I was crazy about this guy and ruined any chance I might have had by acting like a real bitch. I had a lot of growing-up to do. Apparently my near-death experiences had taught me nothing about life, not yet, anyway.

Richard and I got married in July. We quit our jobs and moved out to Phoenix, Arizona. He had gotten a new car, a red Maverick, so we drove cross-country taking our time as honey-mooning tourists.

I got a job with an advertising agency there and he got a job in an auto parts store. After about four or five months of living in an oven, we moved back East. We got a place in Port Washington on Long Island and once again I called Abe to get my job back at Macy's. This time I stayed for a year until I was three months pregnant. I had complications from the pregnancy and had to quit again—this time to stay at home and rest. Among other things, I had toxemia, so bed rest was imperative.

The marriage had lots of problems—mostly drinking problems. Richard was drunk every night. I never drank much and after I became pregnant I didn't drink at all. I smoked, though. Then I discovered that Richard was philandering during (and after my pregnancy). I became depressed and to add to my misery, my father had a heart attack when I was in my eighth month. He survived but never was able to go back to work. His work was ultimately his life. My mother was ill too. They were both too young to die, and because of their bad health, I decided to try and make my marriage work.

IV. DYING TO CHILL OUT

When my daughter was about eleven months old, my father died. Six months later my mother passed away. My father was buried in a cemetery in Queens next to the Expressway. He was with his mother and father.

My mother—they threw away the mold when they made her. She wasn't going to be buried, she had made plans to get FROZEN!

After my father's death, Richard and me and the baby had moved to Virginia, to an area that was a suburb of Washington, D.C. It was 1972. We had been there maybe six weeks when my mother called to say that she was coming down from N.Y. to go into George Washington University Hospital. She had been diagnosed with cancer and had read that GW was a promising place to seek treatment. This was good because GW was only about 40 miles from where I was living.

Cancer... a word which evokes a numbing finality. The awe, the dread, have plagued us for centuries. We can fear spiders or high places and war of nations but the fear of cancer lurks in the crevice of our souls, it stares us down sideways. We don't ponder this thing as we do money, power or sexual fantasies.

Cancer... A Thief. An unconvicted felon who sucks the life-sustaining nutrients from our bodies. This murderer worms its way into the guts of humanity without fear of retribution. It costs us billions of dollars in research, in tantalizing cures, procedures, trials, hopes, misinformation, and final agony. It is finite.

My mother agonized over her demise. She knew her journey into the Cancer World would be her last fantastic voyage and thus, her intellect approached it as such.

At first she spiraled into a dungeon of depression. Perhaps even before the actual diagnosis. In her late forties and early fifties, she became obsessed with the disease. She said that she was going to "get cancer" and she did. It's as though she almost talked herself into it.

My mother was a complicated, creative, educated woman from New York. Born in 1911 to a long-line of hard-working Dutch/German decent Americans. I am told that my grandmother breast-fed her until she was four years old. Her close-knit family included a younger brother, her "mama" and "papa" and a large tree of blossoming cousins.

Her brother, Louie, had cancer.

Uncle Louie was probably in his late twenties when the tumor first presented itself. The details of his disease and his cure are vague. I was a young child at the time and can only recall phrases which alluded to the mysterious malady. My mother's ever-present ego enjoyed taking the credit for his wondrous cure. "If it weren't for me, he would have never been able to have children..." "He would never have gotten married..." How odd. All because of cancer. It was a clandestine melodrama which my mother used as a tool, like a paint brush, to create the aura of her mystique.

As it turned out, Uncle Louie had some form of cancer of the penis. I had always imagined from my mother's ravings, that had she not found this miracle cure—they would have castrated him.

Louie lived to be well into his nineties. My mother, on the other hand, barely made it to sixty, my father—fifty-nine.

I was sucked into remorse and depression when my father died. Too young to die, much too young; and yet, I had no clue, no omen, that my mother would die six months after he did.

The dichotome of the two of them: my father wanted to be cremated and my mother wanted to be frozen. Was he? No. Was she? Sort of.

It was my mother's need to be infinite and immortal that led her to the fantasy of freezing. She abhorred the very idea of death and so she began to explore the world of Cryogenic Suspension in the late sixties.

She had read *The Prospect of Immortality*, by Richard C. W. Ettinger—a book about the scientific search for seemingly eternal life, and she bought it, hook, line and sinker.

When she was admitted to GW in 1972 she had already told me of her plans to get suspended. She had paid for and signed a contract with Cryo-Span Corp (CSC) in New York and had given me and the hospital explicit instructions about what was to be implemented upon her death.

She was to be put immediately on dry ice and then the chilled body was to be transported back to New York where CSC would start the freezing process by performing a perfusion: draining the blood from the body and replacing it with anti-freeze.

After a few weeks the call came. The doctor at GW had called me at night to let me know that my mother had passed away and had been taken to the basement of the hospital to be put on dry ice as CSC had directed them to. I told the doctor that I would take care of the rest of the bizarre procedure.

I had no time to mourn. I was devastated by my mother's passing but also determined to fulfill her dream of getting frozen into eternity and coming back to life once a cure for cancer had been found. My mother was the first known women to have ever attempted this. There had been a few frozen men in New York and California—but no women.

Little did I know that this would turn into a complex fiasco of intrigue involving the MOB, class action law suits, media coverage, and general chaos.

—That was my mother!—

Somehow the media found out about my mother's state, and I was invited to appear on the David Susskind Show (TV) in New York. Along with me, the owner of Cryo Span Corporation, Curtis Henderson, and his assistant, Gillian Cummings, were featured on the talk show.

When I did the show, Susskind asked me a lot of relative questions and then asked me if I was also going to be frozen. "I don't think so. Anyway, you sort of have to be alive when you get frozen for it to work, and if you are frozen while you're still alive—well, that's sort of ... murder." I replied.

Then Jerry Oppenheimer from the *Washington Star* newspaper called me for an interview. The article appeared in the "Metro Life" section on Sunday, August 5, 1973. It was a long interview and an even longer article titled "A Chilling Chance for Immortality."

He starts by saying: "You can, of course, be buried in anything from a pine box to a velvet-lined bronze $10,000 casket. You can be cremated and have your ashes placed in an urn on a loved one's mantel. You can offer your body, or parts thereof, to medical research.

Or, if you have the money and an undying desire for immortality, you can take the still lightly-traveled route the late Mrs. Smith took. Someday, if Mrs. Smith has her way, she'll be back to tell future generations what it was like.

It begins with death.

Shortly before nine o'clock on the morning of last December 10, Mrs. Smith, a teacher and inventor, mother and widow, died at George Washington University Hospital here (Washington, D.C.) after a year-long battle with Leiomyo Sarcoma, a cancerous tumor of the small muscles."

He went on to describe how the body was chilled on dry ice and then transported to New York to CSC. "Today, looking exactly as she did on the day she died, Mrs. Smith is still on ice, dry ice at a cost of about $250.00 a month. She is also wrapped in aluminum foil and rests in an insulated wooden box."

She had been that way for almost eight months because Curtis Henderson didn't have a cryogenic capsule to put her into. These specially designed capsules which eerily emulated the iron lungs that were used for polio victims, had to be special-ordered from Minnesota Valley Engineering Corp., the only company in the U.S. that made them. It had been ordered late in January and was finally completed in August. That's when the fiasco began. Henderson suddenly claimed that he was bankrupt and wanted me to use a company in California.

A few days later, he put me in touch with Robert Nelson AKA Bob "The Freezer" Buccelli from Boston, who was then the President of The Cryogenic Society (TCS) of California. After many telephone conversations, Nelson indicated that he was interested in striking up a deal with me (which was OK with Henderson), but he must "inspect" the body before any commitment was made. To do so, Nelson requested that the Estate pay the round-trip airfare to New York from California. The airfare and a meeting were arranged (although Nelson did show up, it was later revealed that he flew to Boston first to see his mob friends). In order to fly to Boston, he used funds that were initially intended for his transportation to New York.

Nelson arrived to inspect the body: he stated that it was O.K. and that he wanted to freeze the body at his "new" headquarters in Butler, New Jersey (a cemetery). When the capsule for my mother finally arrived, the people running the cemetery called me and stated that they knew nothing about the capsule and that Mr. Nelson was not connected with the cemetery.

For six months, I called and wrote to Nelson; many arguments ensued, and he refused to follow through with the terms of the contract (my mother's body was still wrapped in aluminum foil in a wooden box filled with dry ice; and I was still paying Henderson a monthly fee for all of this).

Gillian Cummings, the VP of CSC, had her father frozen in a capsule at the Long Island location. She tried to supplant her income by selling ice cream from a Good Humor truck. Eventually she ran out of money and committed suicide by freezing herself to death in her ice cream truck.

Ten months after her suicide: my mother's capsule was sitting in Butler, New Jersey, and her body was still on dry ice in New York.

I then got a mysterious phone call from a man in Pennsylvania who said that he had "heard" that I had a nitrogen capsule "for sale". He refused to tell me who told him, but I figured that I no longer had any use for it since the whole thing was hopeless at that point. The man claimed that he needed it immediately for his father who had just died.

I negotiated a price with him and arranged to meet him in a private pilot's lounge at Dulles International Airport at midnight (his request). Several hours prior to the meeting, I received a phone call from Jim Rice, the owner/operator of "Air Hearse", the plane that was to fly the body and his son to Dulles. He stated that an additional passenger was coming along: a Dr. Fahy—a perfusion expert.

At midnight, they all showed up in the lounge. I was given a huge brown paper bag with $3,700.00 in ones and fives. It took me almost 2 hours to count the money. They left the airport and I went home and put the money into my upright piano. It would have been too difficult to explain, had I tried to deposit it into the bank.

At this point—the body was still on dry ice, the capsule had been sold, and there was really no hope of the suspension being a success.

Ultimately, I made the decision to have the body buried and file a lawsuit against Nelson.

I made arrangements for the funeral. I was informed that the body must be "thawed" prior to burial and that the process takes approximately 72 hours.

When I arrived at the cemetery, I was informed that I must identify the body prior to the burial. I was shocked, but agreed to identify the body since I was the Executrix of the Estate. The body looked perfect, almost alive, and at this point the body had been on dry ice for almost a year.

After the burial ceremony I contacted the office of F. Lee Bailey in Beverly Hills, California, and signed a retainer agreement with Richard Rossen, Esq. who agreed to file suit against Robert Nelson and TCS (California).

The case proceeded and a private investigator (Michael Worthington) was hired. After about one year had passed, Worthington discovered that several other people had claims against TCS for thawed bodies and breaches of contract.

Mr. Worthington, in the interim, received his law degree while investigating the case. In 1975, with advice from Mr. Rossen, I turned the case over to Mr. Worthington. Six years later the case went to trial and the final outcome made headlines in the *New York Times*, the *L.A. Times*, and *Newsday*, to name a few.

Robert Nelson later sued his attorney in 1986 (and won) and a minimal settlement was made to me for $700.00. The other parties in the class action have not yet settled and are presumably suing Worthington.

I read through several of the newspapers. This wasn't the kind of publicity that I had planned on getting in my lifetime, but it was, indeed, an extension of my mother's obituary. Some of the articles focused on the lawsuit, such as:

Newsday

—May 28, 1981: **Family Sues Over Deep-Frozen Corpse**

"... three families are suing an organization that deep-froze corpses, including that of a Great Neck woman, in anticipation of future life-restoring treatment.

The Cryonics Society and its chief operator, Robert F. Nelson, are on trial in Los Angeles County Superior Court for allegedly not meeting commitments for continued preservation of the bodies after the non-profit organization ran out of funds..."

New York Times

—June 6, 1981: **$800,000 Awarded By Jury In Suit Over Frozen Dead**

"... a jury has awarded $800,000 in damages to the survivors of three persons whose bodies were frozen because the Cryonics Society of California, which deep-froze dead persons for future revival, allowed the bodies to thaw.

The Superior Court jury returned a verdict yesterday against Robert Nelson, former president of the society, which is now out of business, and Joseph Klockgether, an undertaker."

Collecting that award was a whole other story. Nelson's ties to the mob suggested that the whole thing was a scam, and the whole thing was even more macabre than I could have ever imagined. Strange exhibits popped up during the trial in California and one of them utterly floored me:

It was a dissertation marked “EXHIBIT L”. The title of the 32-page document was:

> “The Perfusion and Freezing of a 60 year-old women”.
> By Gregory M. Fahy, B.S.
> Department of Pharmacology, Medical College of Georgia
> Michael D. Federwicz
> Cyro-Span Corporation, Mid Western Branch

Well, well, well... wasn’t Dr. Fahy, the same Dr. Fahy who came to Dulles Airport on Air Hearse and who was introduced to me as a “perfusion expert? Why, yes, he was. In a numbing awe, I read further; the introduction stated:

> “At 9:25 AM on December 10th, 1972, a 60-year-old hospitalized female patient in Washington, D.C. passed through clinical death. After a 45 minute delay, external cooling of the patient was initiated. The patient was packed in ice and driven to the St. James Funeral Home in St. James, Long Island, arriving there at approximately 10:30 PM. This report documents the effort made to achieve cryophylaxis prior to freezing. To our knowledge, this is the first such account published in open literature. By a complete description of our problems and difficulties, we hope to

> help those involved with future procedures of this kind attain a higher quality operation, in every respect."

Upon reading the entire report, it became apparent to me that these people, without my knowledge or consent, had performed all kinds of examinations (even rectal) on my mother's body. I was livid and disgusted by it. In their discussion they admit:

> "This report represents the first known attempt to scientifically document and analyze an actual perfusion and freezing of a human being. The document includes flow rates, cooling rates, timetable of perfusion, analysis of the effluent samples, and several recommendations for future operations of this sort. Extensive discussion of the case history of this patient is given throughout all phases of the technical operation. Postmortal pathology is discussed."

There was nothing I could do about it when I had found out because I made this discovery more than nine years after she had died.

V. A DIVORCÉE AND A GAY

In 1973 when I was having the nightmare with Robert Nelson, I was also having a domestic war. My husband, besides being plastered most of the time, was back to his "spreading joy among the women of Virginia."

I had hired a detective to make sure that I wasn't being paranoid about his philandering. Well, he was and I wasn't. I had tried and tried and tried to make the marriage work...because of our daughter who was by now 2-1/2 years old and because I needed stability while I was balancing my household responsibilities with the many, many complications of my mother's estate.

After I finally buried my defrosted mother, I also made the decision to bury my marriage ... put it in a casket and shove it six feet under. So I set about finding yet another lawyer.

It was the end of 1973. Things were ending. The Vietnam War was ending. Richard had served in Vietnam in the Air Force, while his mother, to his embarrassment, marched in protest from New York to Washington, D.C.

It was the end of my mother's dream: to get frozen and then come back to life in maybe two hundred years cured of cancer and ready to live in a new society.

I had won a supposedly losing battle against paralytic polio and I had survived falling off a U.S. Naval destroyer ... and an attempted suicide.

Now it was time to end my marriage. Hell, I could survive a divorce!, and I wrote:

The leaves are dying.

Scarlet fever plagues the trees.
And their leaves descend
Upon this earth;
Each mauve hand
A corpse of flowers.

Richard was a violent drunk. That's why I had to leave him. He had thrown me down a flight of steps when I was pregnant and continued to be abusive after we moved to Virginia.

We were renting an attractive two bedroom contemporary apartment in Virginia and I soon became good friends with the two kids that lived upstairs—David and Jim. They lived with their parents on the third floor. Jim was fourteen at the time. A tall lanky fair-haired kid who was very artistic and articulate. David, his brother, was nineteen. He was nothing like Jim. He was exceedingly mature for his age, both in appearance and behavior ... he could have been Jim's father. He was nineteen going on thirty and he looked thirty. He was shorter than Jim, maybe 5'9", with brown hair and large blue soulful eyes that were framed in horn-rimmed glasses. He was pudgy but in an attractive way and he was very grave. He was a 19 year old businessman. When we met he was in the process of negotiating the purchase of an ice cream parlor. It was located in a popular downtown shopping plaza that had an outdoor café and a man-made lake nearby.

This kid put together an unbelievable deal to purchase (and manage) the trendy ice cream store in a matter of months and was soon running the business as though he had been doing this for years.

David and me became good pals. He knew about my problems with Richard and could even hear my screams for help up on the third floor where he lived.

One day when he saw that my arms and face were black and blue, he encouraged me to get a lawyer.

I was on the phone with the Legal Aid Society when Richard came home from work drunk. When he realized who I had been talking to he became enraged and started to smack me around.

They put me in touch with a lawyer named Hal. He was a gentle, intense, understanding man. The first thing he did was to take photos of my bruises which were on my face, arms and hips. Then he set about writing up a separation agreement and a letter to Richard directing him to leave the premises.

Thank god Richard moved out. I was enormously relieved, and even though I had the locks changed, I was still afraid that he'd come and get me or worse, kidnap our daughter which he had threatened to do.

Jim had become my babysitter when I needed one. He was great with my daughter and it worked out very well. Both Jim and David were my closest allies during the separation and divorce.

Richard wasn't making a lot of money at the time. He was in charge of taking care of ice resurfacing at an ice skating rink nearby. He was very proud of driving his Zamboni every few hours over the sliced up and scarred ice at the rink.

I had received enough money from my father's estate to get by for a few years without having to work and I really wanted to be a stay-at-home mother until my daughter was maybe four years old. Most of the time I was paying all of our bills anyway. What Richard kept for himself he used for his drinking and his escapades with women. I had finally gotten a car after my father died—a 1972 chocolate brown Pinto hatchback. I bought it new for about two thousand dollars (and gas was only 35¢ a gallon, and cigarettes were 50¢ a pack).

I told Hal that I was really scared of Richard and he told me that I could not get a restraining order until another attack occurred and I called the police and documented it.

It was the beginning of August. David came down one afternoon and told me that he was going to sell his ice cream parlor and go to college to get a business degree. "That seems like a good idea, where would you go to school? Northern Virginia Community College?"

"No" he said, "I'm going to a Community College in West Palm Beach.":

"What!?" This was news to me. Apparently he had already applied and had been accepted, and the ice cream parlor was on the market.

"When are you going?" "The end of August. Why don't you come down to Florida with me? Just disappear so Richard can't find you?"

Well, now that's an idea, I thought, and I thought and I thought and I waved it around in my mind like a white flag.

"O.K. Let's take the Auto Train!"

I called Hal and told him about my plan. He said that was alright and that he wouldn't tell Richard where I was because of client confidentiality. I figured I'd put my stuff in storage and rent a furnished apartment.

About a week after we had left, Jim called me to let me know that Richard tried to break down the door at the apartment. When he realized he couldn't break it down he hired a locksmith. Apparently, after he got in and saw all of the furniture gone, he went bonkers and punched out a few walls.

I got a small garden apartment on the Lake in West Palm Beach. David was staying at the dorm at the school he was going to.

After about a month, David decided that he hated the school and wanted to go back to Virginia, which he did.

I was sad to see him go. He had been a very supportive friend. I hung in there until November, until I realized that I'd soon be running out of money. I wasn't after child support from Richard, I just never wanted to see him again. I didn't want any ties because I was terrified of him.

I decided to go back to the Washington area and try to find a part-time job. My daughter was 3 by then, fully toilet-trained and very expressive for her age. But I couldn't go to Virginia because of Richard, so I took the Auto Train back and drove to Maryland.

David was a great help. He aided me in finding an apartment, getting my stuff out of storage, and unpacking. He wound-up coming out to my place in Maryland every weekend.

Our age difference never phased me. He was my best friend, my pal, and I needed him and he needed me. Somehow, and I don't *know* how, we wound up in bed together.

David had always hinted around that he was gay and I had accepted that, plus I was almost 10 years older than him. He had even told me that he had had a male lover, but apparently, at this stage of his life, he was *sort-of* bi-sexual, if there is such a thing.

The sex was good. It wasn't as wild and unabandoned as my affair with Bert in San Juan, but it was there. It was *better* than a wham-bam, thank-you, ma'am. We kissed, fondled, got steamy, and came. He accepted it and I accepted it.

I got my daughter into a good day care center near my apartment in Maryland and I went into Washington, D.C. looking for a job. I wanted something part-time because leaving my daughter after more than 3 years together was heart-wrenching. Oh, how we both cried on that first day apart. We had very entwined apron strings.

I lucked out. After poring over the want-ads in *The Washington*

Post, I applied for a job as Assistant Manager/Hostess at Duke Zeibert's Restaurant in Washington. The pay was good and the hours were perfect. The only problem was that I had no restaurant experience.

I made an appointment to meet with the manager, Mel Krupin, and I lied like hell. I told him that I had just moved down from New York and used to work at a restaurant on Long Island, and I named a popular restaurant in Great Neck.

"Well, I'll be damned!." Mel blurted out while sucking on a huge phallic-like cigar. He had such a thick Brooklyn accent that I should have known that he was from New York.

"Y'know, I usta be a butcher in New Yawk. I usta be the meat supplia for dat place... I don't remember you—I woulda remembered *you*, kiddo."

"I used to work at night there."

Duke Zeibert's was hot. It had a back room called "Allen's Alley" which was reserved for Coach Allen and the Washington Redskins. The politicians went there and the C.I.A. hung out at the bar.

I was never really into politics at that time and knew nothing about sports. One afternoon, Mel invited me to sit at a table with some chunky red-haired guy who was chewing on a cigar. He was being interviewed by a loud-mouthed guy from the media. Mel introduced me to the guys and they asked me to join them. It was after lunch hour, maybe 3 o'clock. The red-head introduced himself to me again and we shook hands. I said, "Hi." Then, suddenly he laughed and said, "You don't know who I am, *do* you?" "No." He laughed some more. "And you don't know who this guy is either, do you?" (while elbowing the guy next to him). "No." They both thought that this was pretty funny.

As it turned out, I was sitting with Sonny Jurgenson and Howard Cosell.

That night I called David to tell him about what happened. I still wasn't too sure who Sonny and Howard were and when I told David, well *he* started laughing, too.

By this time my divorce was final and I was making enough money to make ends meet. David and I were still part-time lovers which meant that we made love *very* infrequently. I suspected that he was seeing some guy on the side, too.

I had been working at Duke's for about half a year by then. My daughter was four and I was finally living life, and then I got pregnant.

I was horrified. I really didn't want a child at that time in my life. David seemed proud and happy. He vowed to stand-by me. What gay wouldn't?

"I won't marry you, but I'll support the baby."

Hell, I didn't want to *marry* him, whether I was pregnant or not. We went around in circles for a month about what to do. At that time he was the head accountant for a Toyota dealership in Virginia. At the same time, Mel Krupin confronted me. "You know, you're pretty good at what you do—you're da best gal we've had in a long time. But you're no restaurant person. Hell, ya didn't even know what a "four-top" was when I hired you—but you're a good-looker and I tooka chance." "What are you, really?"

I told him. I told him that I was an advertising artist and I used to work at Macy's in New York.

"Christ! I can get you a real job where you can do your thing—I'm great friends with Alvin Erlich!"

I didn't know who Alvin Erlich was but I thought, O.K., I'll see where this goes.

A few days later I was sitting in Alvin's office in Bethesda, Maryland with my portfolio. It took twenty minutes.

"Can you start on Monday?" "I've gotta give Mel notice..." "I've already notified him, don't worry about it."

I felt sad leaving Duke's. It was like my family. I loved the power players who came through the revolving doors on L Street every day and the clandestine meetings in the bar, the cigar smoke, the TV cameras roaming around looking for hot shots. I had become friends with Randy, Duke's son who worked the front door with me. I had felt sorry for him when Duke would humiliate him in front of everyone. Generally, he referred to Randy as, "You idiot..." Randy once tried to console me by saying, "Don't let it bother you—it's just the way he is."

A week after starting my new job at Alvin's Agency, I miscarried. Another death to contend with. I thought by this time I was truly hardened by tragedy. But I wasn't really. I sank back down into one of my deep depressions and missed a lot of work.

Eventually I got fired. David and I were still friends but we never had sex after that. He was pretty honest about it... "I'm really more comfortable with men..."

I met Bob just in time. It was by then, 1978. I was at a disco in D.C. called the "Appletree", it *was* the place to go in the 70's and I absolutely loved Disco. In fact I wound up with the sobriquet of "Disco Baby" after many nights of partying at the Appletree on 19th Street and Elan on K Street.

Bob was a Lawyer at the Veteran's Administration in D.C. He lived in Virginia and took the Metro to work because he didn't have a car, so in order to see him on weekends I had to drive to Virginia, pick him up and drive him back to Maryland to my place. He would end up spending the weekend and taking the train to work on Monday morning.

At that time I was working at a magazine in McLean, Virginia as the Art Director. I would design the magazine and put together ads as they came in. My little office on the top floor of the building was across the hall from an office that had "AFIA" on the door. I watched as middle-aged men in safari shirts with button down shoulder tabs would go in and out of that door. Some of these guys would stop by my office to chat and flirt and loiter. I discovered that "AFIA" stood for Association of Former Intelligence Officers. These guys were spooks! I should have known because the office building was on Whittier Avenue ... about 2 blocks from C.I.A. Headquarters ... and Chuck Colson—Nixon's former aide-turned-born-again-Christian—had an office downstairs.

What a hoot!

On staff with the magazine was a formidable guy who was a Dining Critic. Warren was a "they threw away the mold" character. His nickname was either "Commander Whitehead" or "Mr. Schwepps"—whichever you liked.

Warren was in his sixties, tall, thin and agile. He sported a sculpted white beard and mustache with thin white hair on his scalp. The restaurants in Northern Virginia all had his dining reviews hanging on their vestibule walls. He'd been with the *Journal Newspapers* for years and fancied himself as a competitor of Phyllis Richman, a renowned Washington critic.

We became fast friends. Sometimes Warren, Bob and me would go to the disco's in D.C. on Saturday nights and party the night away.

Bob and Warren got along pretty well considering that Bob was a liberal Democrat from Boston and Warren was a border-line Neo-Nazi.

My relationship with Bob was good. It surely wasn't the love of my life but we had predictable, fulfilling sex, including a smattering of oral exploitations which I quickly came to enjoy.

VI. THE ADVERTISING AGENCY

I left the magazine because they were apparently running out of money. On more than a few occasions my pay check bounced and that's when I knew that it was bail-out time. And I saw an opportunity where I lived in Maryland.

The local Holiday Inn had been looking for a small ad agency to handle their print and media marketing. I met with the General Manager and we immediately hit it off. Jim was an arrogant Greek descended guy in his 50's, who had retired from the Navy. His office displayed walls of photos of him with President Johnson, Pierre Salinger and other White House notables, as well as awards, medals and letters from dignitaries. After leaving the Navy he was the General Manager for the Holiday Inn in Morocco. He fascinated me. It was odd that his wife was the Housekeeping Director of the Inn, a dowdy, thin, quiet, background kind of woman. From what Jim said, their marriage was good and he would often remark about their avid bed-life. (I thought, *yeah*, right!).

What made Jim so attractive was a combination of his assertiveness and his utter charm. We would often have our meetings in the lounge that was in the basement of the inn. At one point, we actually renamed the lounge and it became the "Crystal Palace", and he had me designing new logos, signage, bar menus, ads for the local papers, and writing and producing radio spots.

At last, I was where I wanted to be. I was a working mother and in charge of my life and my successful little business. My baby advertising firm was moving along and I finally got to go a little crazy with my radio spots, like using "Bolero" by Ravel, in my commercial for the Crystal Palace.

Jim appreciated my creativity and nurtured it, and although he loved to flirt with me and have naughty thoughts (no doubt), he kept the relationship on a professional level.

The Taubman Corporation was building a mall across the street from the Holiday Inn. This small town had basically two things going for it then: the Holiday Inn and the large IBM complex up the street. Now, a major mall was being built.

Jim called me one day to let me know that Al Taubman (President of the Taubman Corporation) was staying in the Presidential Suite at the Inn and that he had his personal helicopter parked on the Inn's roof.

He said he wanted me to come over to his office and meet a young lady—Nancy—who was the Marketing Director of the Mall.

There, sitting behind Jim's desk was a petite, bubbly, attractive blonde. Nancy was from Dallas, Texas, and everyone's name to her was "Darlin". She was sternly professional, stating precisely what her needs and expectations were. At first I was a little intimidated by her—her enormous self-assurance, her somewhat demanding professionalism. Nancy was about the same age as me and in some odd way reminded me of Harriett, my high school class president.

At the end of the meeting she assured me, "I'll be in touch, I'm interviewing a few other companies to handle our advertising." I wanted this account. With my retail background from Macy's and Nancy's hints at her support for women's lib, I thought I had a good shot at it.

She got up and walked around the desk to shake my hand. I was stunned to see that she was limping. She had that familiar roll to her walk that I had witnessed hundreds of times at the Sister Kenney Institute. I tried not to gape at her, but then I blurted out, "Did you have polio?"

She acted surprised, and I can't blame her. Who the hell would blurt-out such a thing? Well, me, obviously. There was a ghastly moment of silence.

"Yeas", she drawled, sounding a lot like my former roommate, Corky, who was also from Texas.

"I did, too." She kind of looked at me in disbelief probably because I had no noticeable disability. "I was at the Sister Kenny Institute in New Jersey for almost a year." She told me that she had spent some time in a hospital in Texas. She was about three when she had polio. That was probably what contributed to the different levels of our rehabilitation. At nine years old, my muscles were more developed than hers were at three. She told me about her treatments which were similar to mine, but she had had several operations as well. As I got to know her, I could see that there was some bitterness, a longing to be like the other kids.

But she had done extraordinarily well. She had completed college in Texas and her roommate there had been Farrah Fawcett (unknown at that time). She had been with the Taubman Corporation for a number of years and held a job with a very high position of authority.

We chatted briefly about polio and then the meeting was over. It was hard for me to figure out how I had fared; whether or not I had a shot at getting the account. I thought that I might have screwed-up by asking her about polio. Later, Jim and me talked about it down in the Crystal Palace. He was very discouraging. He was sure that I blew it and kind of reprimanded me in a fatherly way.

That evening I called David. We were still buddies and he had good instincts when it came to business. At one point I had introduced him to Jim and they hated each other. Jim had a *real* distaste for gays and David had a *real* animosity towards "macho, right-wing ex-Navy fighter pilots" which is how he had referred to Jim.

And, David's theory was just the opposite. He ventured that I got the account because he suspected that deep down, Nancy needed an ally and besides my heavy retail background, he felt that a strong part of my personality was in forming lasting friendships both in business and on a personal level.

Although Jim had been negative, he was delighted that I got the account. Yes! I thought. Yes, yes, yes! I was thrilled. My infant agency was hired to do the Mall's grand-opening as well as the following year's promotions. The local paper did a business blitz about me, photo and all.

This was no small account and it took considerable time to work on: I was writing and designing all the print ads, writing and producing all of the radio spots, and writing all of the Press Releases. As if that weren't enough, Nancy had me doing all of the media buys as well, which was great, because that was agency commissionable. I was also handling the Holiday Inn account and had a few other "free-lance" type accounts, too, like an occasional job for Riggs Bank of Washington, Paine-Webber, General Solar Corp. and WWDC-FM radio where Howard Stern was working at the time. Later on, I acquired my good old buddy, Duke Zeibert's restaurant when they opened their new place on Connecticut Avenue. *That* was another awesome account.

But my primary account then was the Mall and the Grand Opening event which took all of my time and energy. I planned a remote broadcast by WMAL Radio featuring their popular duo "Harden & Weaver"; with that came the press releases and the radio and print campaign. I was on a roll.

Nancy and me became good friends and I invited her along with me, Bob, and Warren to go partying downtown at Club Elán. Even with her disability, Nancy somehow compensated and was a pretty good disco dancer. She was really a *master* of compensation, and although she would occasionally fall, she would laugh and pick herself up and start all over again.

It was the fall of 1979. My daughter was eight years old by then and in the third grade. She was an excellent and popular student and went to a day care program after school. The school, my apartment, the Holiday Inn and the Mall were all within one-half mile of each other, so this proximity gave me great flexibility.

My relationship with Bob had become strained by then. With all this going on in my life, he still expected me to be his personal chauffeur. The drive to his place in Virginia and back to Maryland took almost two hours. He had a driver's license and could have easily rented a car to alleviate the strain; the strain being that I often had to spend at least half of the weekend working.

I had my office set-up in my apartment. When I first got the Holiday Inn account I decided to sell my dining room furniture and buy office furniture. I got a big desk, a chair and a file cabinet, as well as a "Mayline Board", which is a desk-top drafting table, and I bought an abundance of drafting supplies. I got an answering service for my telephone and designed business cards, letterheads and invoices for my company.

I now had a one-man advertising firm in my dining room. Who knew that I would wind-up in "Who's Who?" Bob was very supportive of this and he had a wry, Irish sense of humor (and freckles, to boot) but it had become stale and we finally parted ways before Thanksgiving.

I had the Thanksgiving and Christmas promos to work on then. We had actually started the planning in September, and I had a lot of promos to attend, as well. I went to special events at the Holiday Inn and at other malls, to ad club meetings in Washington, D.C., and of course, to discos for a little diversion. I often went with Warren, the distinguished dining critic or with a group including Nancy, other Taubman

PR execs and with Warren's friend, Jack, a Virginia attorney, and sometimes with the media—Tony from WGMS, Rick from WYRE, and the Adler brothers from the *Washington Dossier*. I wasn't seeing much of David because he had been caught in one of his sophisticated schemes and had been indicted for embezzling thousands of dollars from the Toyota Car Dealership he had been working for. He got sent to the "White Collar" detention facility on the beach in Florida. Later, a couple of years later, he told me that he really liked the place. He said he spent his days playing golf and lolling by the ocean and that the food wasn't too bad and he had found a lover there for the duration. I was sad for him and I was happy for him. He had come to terms with his homosexuality and was paying the price for being greedy.

I, on the other hand, continued to be straight (sexually) and honest in business. I probably wasn't charging enough for the Mall Account, but I was glad to be doing so well. I threw a nice Christmas party at the end of '79, renting a small auxiliary room at the Shoreham-Americana Hotel in Washington. It was basically a client/media business bash for the purpose of drumming up good PR for my company. I had an open bar with hors d'oeuvres and a DJ doing disco. There were about seventy people in attendance and it was a great success.

That's when I started toying with the idea that I needed a bigger apartment. I thought maybe one with 3 bedrooms and I'd use one bedroom as an office.

I had been living in the same place for six years. It was nice—two bedrooms and two baths. My daughter was friends with all of the kids there and I was well-acquainted with my neighbors. Jo and her two boys across the hall, Charlie and Margaret upstairs, the "spider-women" and her two kids above me (she used to come down and kill spiders in my apartment for me—I have arechnophoebia— and Susan next door. It was an at-home-single-mom support group in a sense, except for Charlie and Margaret.

They were in their early sixties. They had moved to the apartment complex after Charlie had been laid-off from NASA. He had been their Marketing Director. NASA's cut-backs were an integral part of the news then. Basically, the government was cutting back on their space programs and in a situation like that, marketing was always the first thing to get bumped. They had sold their large house and put a lot of things in storage. Margaret was working at a retail store as an Interior Decorating Consultant and Charlie sat at home waiting for NASA to call.

Charlie began drinking the minute Margaret left for work. He was usually plastered by twelve noon. Since I had an in-home office, I was home a lot. Sometimes Charlie would stop by to visit and chat. He was an interesting guy, an intellect who needed the stimulus of his career, without it he found oblivion in his bottle. He napped in the afternoon and was almost sober when Margaret came home and then they had their before-dinner-cocktails together and the cycle started over again.

I had introduced Charlie to Warren thinking they would hit-it-off. Warren being the distinguished neo-Nazi, Martini-guzzler, and Charlie, the politically conservative William Buckleyish cerebral alcoholic. They got along in a very competitive, intellectualesque manner, often arguing about Ezra Pound, of all things.

In the early Spring of 1980, I began to think seriously of getting a larger apartment to accommodate my business. I wanted to stay close to where I was so my daughter could remain at the same school and I could be near the Holiday Inn and the Mall.

I contacted a real estate agent and told her my parameters. There were lots of apartments available then. The area was a new community with the usual amenities: a man-made lake, rows of townhouses, a golf course, an area with larger, expensive homes and contemporary garden-style apartments, and, of course, the new Mall. She showed me a variety of nice spaces and late in May I zeroed into an apartment right behind the Holiday Inn. It had two bedrooms, two baths and a large windowed den with a door. This den was perfect for my office. The only drawback was that I had to talk myself into accepting the red wall-to-wall carpeting. It was *really* red. It was also on the third floor, a walk-up, which I thought was a plus. I had always felt a little uncomfortable at the apartment I had been living in because it was at ground level and I had envisioned how easy it would have been for someone to break-in. So this unit on the third floor seemed safer to me..it was just that damn red carpet.

The place was actually a condominium and I would be renting from the owner. But that was okay because the rent included the condo fees and utilities and it was within my budget.

"I think I found a new apartment near the mall", I was telling Charlie. "Maybe you and Margaret could come and look at it before I sign the lease?" I could just imagine what Margaret's reaction to the red carpet would be.

Charlie and Margaret were like surrogate parents to me. We had lived in the same building together for more than five years and their opinion mattered to me.

"Oh, my Loord!" I knew Margaret would say that when she saw the carpet. "Well, that room back there is just perfect for an office...and the kitchen's nice—all new appliances. I like the layout, but are you sure you want to be up three flights? "Yeah, I feel safer on a high floor and look, there's a view of the lake."

On our way out of the building, I noticed a guy standing about 15 feet from the entrance. It wasn't his eyes that I felt, even though he was leering at me; it was the presence of his pervasive emotion. As we walked down the steps I was suddenly aware of an evil aura, a hawk-like menace near me. "Did you see that guy! He was a real creep" I commented to Margaret. I made a mental note of the feeling as we left the place. I had sensed a tortured, twisted animal lurking near me, an animal that was stalking his prey.

We drove back to our apartment complex and I forgot about the incident. I made a deal to lease the unit and the owners said that I could move in on June 1. I arranged for the movers to come on June 3rd. In the interim, I was taking boxes of things over there each day in my spare time. It was very quiet there during the week because most of the tenants were at work. I had a very foreboding feeling when I went there. I couldn't explain it, but I felt like someone was watching me.

I told Jim, the GM of the Holiday Inn about the creep I had seen loitering at the new apartment. I suppose I told him because I knew he'd think that it was "kinky" and kinky appealed to him. "What did he look like?"

"Well, he's a little shorter than me , maybe 5'7" or 5'8". He was dark, maybe Latin; he was wearing jeans and a jacket and maybe in his twenties. He was very focused, he was staring at me. I could feel his eyes on me—he *really* gave me the creeps." Jim laughed.

I felt that I was being very paranoid, so I didn't discuss the creep with anyone else, and I deliberately forget about it.

VII. IT'S A CRIME

Finally, it was June third...moving day. I had everything packed and was totally ready for the move but there was one problem, my daughter woke up feeling sick that morning and she had a fever. I decided to keep her home from school and let her rest while the movers were working and when they were done I could take her to the doctor. That was the plan.

It was after one o'clock in the afternoon when the movers finally took up the last boxes and pieces of furniture to the new apartment. We were tired and hungry, so I locked-up the place and took my daughter to the nearby Sir Walter Raleigh Inn—a popular restaurant chain in Maryland and Virginia. I really liked their salad bar. It was always fresh and had a particular kind of thousand island dressing that was very good. It was nice to finally relax after moving. The stress of moving isn't just the physical labor, but the trauma of a new environment, and I also had to deal with my daughter's illness which didn't seem to be improving.

When we got back to the apartment I called her pediatrician whose office was only a few blocks away. The doctor couldn't see my daughter until four o'clock. That gave me some time to bring up a few boxes I had in the car. I told my daughter to rest in her room and she could watch her TV until it was time to go to the doctor, while I went down to the car to get the boxes.

When I finally finished lugging the boxes up the three flights of stairs it was getting close to 3:45 p.m. so I told my daughter to get her shoes on, it was time to go. I was standing in the dining room while she sat on the living room floor tying her shoes. I was thinking about how the red carpet didn't really look so bad after all and then there was a very strong hand on my mouth...in a flash I thought it was my daughter playing a game, but she was standing right in front of me....

I wrenched this thing off of my mouth: this hand that was like a blood sucker gripping my face, I yanked it away and screamed at the top of my lungs, knowing that someone was behind me, and was going to do only God knows what. It was all in a split second and then I could feel the icy edge of the knife on my throat and he was saying, "Shut-up or I'll kill you..." I *did* shut-up and then he slashed me across the mouth with the knife. I started to bleed profusely. I didn't want my daughter to see this. I wanted to protect her from this monster who had invaded my life and who had slashed my face. I suspected that it was going to be a rape so I said, "Whatever you want, you can't do this in front of my daughter..." "Okay, okay"...and pulling my arm, with the bloody knife now pointed at her, he directed her to her room, and she obeyed, thank *God*.

"Where's the money?" "It's in my pocketbook...in the living room..." I blubbered. I was "blubbering" because my lips were falling off my face from being slashed and it was difficult to talk. It felt like having three sets of lips and not being able to control any of them and blood was oozing down my neck, warm like maple syrup.

I had only twenty dollars. I showed him my wallet. "That's all I have!" "Take off our pants.!" Oh God, I thought, this is it, this is the real reason that he's here, it isn't really a robbery. I took off my pants. "Take everything off..." I started removing my underwear and I said to him as he was staring at my pubic hair, "My daughter's doctor is due here any minute...you must have heard me on the phone...if you don't leave you're going to get caught..." "Okay, okay.." and then he left.

I was in a total state of shock. I was still bleeding profusely...I pulled my pants back on and ran to the door and bolted it. Then my daughter came into the living room crying," Mommy, Mommy..."

"It's okay. It's okay." I said calmly. But I was far from calm. I ran to the phone and dialed 911. I could barely talk but I told them my address and that I had been knifed and I begged them to stay on the phone with me until help arrived.

It was the creep. The creep who had been hiding in the shadows when I showed the apartment to Charlie and Margaret, the creep that I had told Jim about.

The rescue squad arrived but I was so terrified at that point that I wouldn't let them in. I thought the creep might still be on the other side of the door. "Maam let us in—we're here to help you." "Do you have any I.D...Hold your I.D. up to the peephole..."

After a few minutes of hesitation I finally let them in. They quickly taped the slashes on my face to stop the bleeding. As they started asking me questions, they put me on a stretcher and started to carry me out of the building. "My daughter!," I screamed. "Where's my daughter?" "She's right here, Maam." "She's sick, she's running a fever, she needs to be treated, too."

They took us in an ambulance to a nearby Adventist Hospital. The hospital was fairly new. I had never been there before. I was rushed into a brightly lit operating room. There were several people in attendance—some nurses, an orderly and two surgeons. They took my daughter to another room to take her temperature and let her rest during my surgery.

First they had to take the tape off of my face. That's when I was jarred back to reality and started to feel the pain from the knife wounds. The doctors explained, after inserting an IV, that they were going to inject some kid of pain killer like novocaine into my cheeks and then they were going to try to sew up the slashes on both sides of my mouth. That's when I blurted out: "It's like an episiotomy of the mouth!" The one doctor moaned, and said, "Oh, God!" I guess they were glad to see that I had a sense of humor. Later, a psychiatrist told me that it wasn't humor—it was repressed hysteria.

When they were done and it seemed like a couple of hours later, they finally allowed me to reconnect with my daughter. This poor child had been left alone in a room and was in a state of total fear. She had no idea where her mommy was until I finally walked into her room. She looked at me in horror. Both sides of my face had thick, black stitches going from my mouth straight back to my ears. I must have looked like an ogre.

Then we were taken to another area of the hospital where two detectives were waiting to interview us. I was exhausted, and in a state of shock, but I complied with their requests knowing that they had to do this in order to nab the perpetrator.

"Is there someplace where I can have a cigarette?" "Yeah, there's a lounge over there." All three of us lit up. My face was numb from the anesthetic that they had injected into my cheeks. I tried to inhale and it felt like I had been to the dentist and my lips were like rubber, but I smoked anyway.

"Do you want to call someone to come and get you? Your parents?" the detective with the badge that said 'Neville' asked me. "My parents are dead" I replied flatly. Amazingly, my daughter wasn't crying. She was quietly listening and taking it all in. I'm sure she felt a little more secure while we were with the two detectives. Who to call? I thought. I didn't really have anyone, but I wasn't going back to that apartment and the detectives said I couldn't go back right then because it was still a crime scene. Charlie and Margaret. I'll call them, I thought. God, I hope they're home. By now it was about 8:30 p.m. I had given Neville and his partner a description of the attacker and they had also interviewed my daughter.

Margaret answered the phone. I quickly told her what happened and told her where I was. She said she and Charlie would pick me up at the hospital within a half an hour. "Oh, and could you bring me a shirt or something? The one I'm wearing is all full of blood." "Yes, I'll bring you something to wear." Margaret was great, she was very calm and in control.

When they got to the hospital, she handed me a shirt to wear and I went into the Ladies' Room to change. I threw the blood-soaked shirt that I was wearing into the trash can. When I came out, the other Detective whose name was Williams, asked me where my shirt was." I threw it out—I don't want it anymore." "Oh, no, you can't do that—it's evidence." How would *I* know that? So I went back and got it and gave it to them.

Later, at Charlie's and Margaret's apartment, my daughter went right to sleep in their guest room. The antibiotics that they had given to her at the hospital were taking affect and out she went. Me? Well, I was another story. Margaret went to bed around 10 p.m. and Charlie and I stayed up and chatted. I was near hysteria. I was afraid that my attacker had followed us there and I kept checking the lock on the front door and peering out into the dark parking lot. Charlie was having a nitecap and made me one, too. He could see that I was really shaken by the assault and that I wasn't calming down.

I didn't go to bed until 2 a.m. and even then, I was just drowsing, sitting upright in the bed next to my sleeping daughter. It would take years for me to get a normal sleep after that.

The next day, the detectives called to say that I could go back to the apartment to remove any clothes or things that I wanted to take with me. I had already told them that I would never go back and *live* there. I called the real estate agent to let her know why I was breaking the lease.

The owners of the condo were horrified when they found out what had happened and no one gave me a problem about my breaking the contract.

Even though the police would be at the apartment when I went to get my things, I couldn't bear going alone. I called my neo-Nazi buddy, Warren, and told him what had happened. I asked him to meet me at the apartment the following day and I also said, "Would you bring your Luger?" I needed to feel safe, I needed to be carrying a gun in my purse. He said he would bring his big, German Luger.

Warren picked me up at Charlie and Margaret's apartment. My car was still parked at the new apartment. There were two squad cars sitting out front. Warren had given me the pistol and it *just* fit in my purse. A Luger was a large gun dating back to World War II, which is when Warren got it, while he was in the Army.

The police let us into the unit and I worked as quickly as I could, packing a couple of suitcases for me and my daughter, and being sure to take my portfolio as well.

When this whole fiasco, this attempted murder, had occurred, I was working on two new accounts. I was going to lose the Mall account soon because Nancy had quit her job with The Taubman Corporation. The new Marketing Director of the Mall had announced that she was going to use an agency she had worked with for several years and that my talents weren't an option. So I had been scrambling to land new accounts right before I moved.

I had picked up two: A company that produced printed forms for businesses and Riggs Bank of Washington. For the bank, I was writing and designing a brochure for bank customers which was an introduction of the new ATM system. I still had a couple of months to work on it, so I wasn't worried about that one. But the business form company needed their camera-ready art completed the day after I went back to the apartment with Warren.

After I finished packing the suitcases, the police helped me put it all in my car. I had also called the movers back and told them to go back and take all my stuff—clothing, furniture, everything, out of the apartment and put it into storage.

When they were done, I got into my car and Warren into his and we drove to a nearby restaurant to have lunch.

Warren wanted his Luger back, so I passed the big gun to him under the table at the restaurant and he put it into his briefcase.

"You didn't really think I *loaded* that thing, did you?" he remarked.

Jeez! I thought it was loaded. I really did. But his understandable theory was that you never give an hysterical woman a *loaded* gun!

That night, I wrote:

In trenches of dismay
I fight evil attack;
My war of every day
Piles death on my back.

My breath of every night
inhales the poisoned wind.
I run in secret fright
although I have not sinned.

We were still staying with Charlie and Margaret. The day after I borrowed Warren's Luger and got my stuff out of the apartment, I called the client who needed his business form designs. I had finished them that night at Margaret's desk in the apartment and I wanted to turn the work in on time and get paid.

When I called this client, I warned him that I had been attacked; that I was a victim of a crime, and that my face had been slashed. When I arrived at his office, which was maybe eight miles away from the Holiday Inn, the business form client didn't even blink an eye when he saw me. He just reviewed the work that I had done for him and then handed me a check, very formal, very business-like.

I was beginning to understand how people with pronounced disabilities get treated—they basically get ignored because most people don't know how to deal with it.

I was really still in a state of shock. I looked over my shoulder wherever I went and locked the bedroom door at Charlie and Margaret's house when I went to sleep. But I never slept. I drowsed until it was dawn. On day four I had to decide what I was going to do. My daughter only had a couple of weeks of school left but I couldn't stay around there anymore.

"Janet, it's me. Please sit down. I was knifed and robbed a couple of days ago after I moved into my new apartment..." "Oh, my God!" she gasped noticeably. "Are you O.K.?" "Yeah, sort of. Look, they haven't caught the guy and I want to get out of the area for awhile, and I'll need to go to a doctor to have these stitches taken out of my face. Can we stay with you and Ken for awhile?"

"Oh my God, of course!"

My mother grew up with Janet. They were cousins, but they were as close as two sisters. When my mother died, Janet and her husband, Ken, took on the role of being my parents. They lived in a remote area of Long Island near Cold Spring Harbor.

After my divorce, I would go there, with my daughter, for Thanksgiving and then again for a few days in the Spring or Summer. I knew that we would feel comfortable and safe at her house.

"I'm going to stay with my cousins in New York for awhile." I was telling Margaret and Charlie. They wanted us to stay with them, but I explained how nervous I was in that area. They had been very gracious to me and helped me as much as they possibly could, but I had to get away. I packed what few things we had and hit the road the next day. I took the interstate all the way, averaging 70-80 MPH. I didn't even care about the fact that I looked like a freak with the large black stitches on both sides of my mouth. I didn't care about my company or anything else for that matter. I was focused on the safety of my daughter and me.

I could smell Long Island Sound which was shrouded in purple dusk. Janet's house with its pink shutters, and sweeping lawn, was shaded by large pine trees and rested at the top of a hill. At the bottom of the hill was a little private beach with a white gate and a small planked pier where you could dive or go fishing. Ken often went down to the beach to dig for mussels and to chat with the neighbors. He had been retired for a few years and was in his late sixties. This was a happy man. Playing golf made him very happy and he dressed happy. He would wear pink Bermuda shorts with a lime-green izod knit shirt or bright plaid shorts with a pink shirt and when he went out, even to do errands, he wore a made-to-order rug. Even though the hair that he had on the sides and on the nape of his neck was gray, he wore a dark auburn hairpiece. It was more than just obvious. But he had a good sense of humor about it and said that he wore it to keep his head warm. When he was at home it was the first thing to come off. Janet was a couple of years older than Ken. She had a Barbara Bush body with an unwrinkled, elegant face. She was of Dutch decent and still had her blonde hair which she wore short and beauty-parlor permed. She had worked for her father's company a few years after her only daughter was born, and then was a stay-at-home mom. Janet was a strong woman who held the family together.

When we arrived, I was exhausted. Janet decided to put me and my daughter upstairs in the master bedroom. I was extremely grateful. She apparently sensed how fearful I was and felt that I would feel safer on the second floor. Well, it was true. I was still very traumatized and during the two months I stayed there, I locked the bedroom door every night *and* wedged a chair under the doorknob.

After a fairly decent rest that night (which for me was about two hours of sleep), Janet asked me a ton of questions about the attempted murder. I told her everything that I knew and how I suspected it was the guy I had seen at the apartment a week before I moved in. I told her about the surgery on my face and mentioned again that I needed to go to a doctor to have the stitches removed.

During all this time, she had been taking notes. She took notes in shorthand as though we were at a board meeting. She said she would call one of her doctors for me that afternoon.

"Don't you think you should go into therapy?" I knew she would bring that up. She was big on psychiatrists and had her daughter going to one for years. I declined. She protested. "You *really* have to have therapy, you *know* you have to." "Well, not right now...OK?"

I heard a lot about the therapy from her. I don't know why I refused to go, but for two months she pushed me to try it.

I gave it a lot of thought and concluded that the two reasons I resisted treatment were basically because I had no medical insurance and

I felt that if I could work this out with myself I'd be stronger, emotionally. It was a real tough road. My daughter seemed to be doing okay and I was very careful not to let my fear show.

We spent about eight weeks living in this calm, lulling environment by the beach. We'd have afternoon teas out in the white gazebo on the back lawn and barbequed steak and grilled corn on the cob for dinner. I'd help Janet with the house chores as much as she would let me, and my daughter would play with their enormous black cat, "Licorice".

On weekends there were beach parties and we'd visit Grandpa (Janet's father) who lived in the house across the street.

The phone was ringing. Janet answered it. I was upstairs. She called up to me. Who would be calling me there? Not too many people knew where I was. "Hello?" "Hi, It's Bruce. How are you doing?" "Bruce! How'd you find me?"

It was a long story, and he explained how he tracked me down. He knew what had happened to me and knew why I was staying in New York. Bruce was the Marketing Director of Riggs Bank in Washington, D.C. He wanted me to finish the brochure that I was writing and designing for the introduction of the new ATM machines. It had to be done by September.

He was pleading with me to come back. "Bruce, all of my stuff is in storage, I have no place to live, and I'm not sure if I'm ready yet."

"Well, what about your daughter? Where's she going to go to school in September?"

We had a long discussion about the work and my circumstances. Finally I said that I'd have to think about it, and I'd call him back.

I had known Bruce for a few years. I actually had met him through David's brother: Jim, the one who used to babysit for me. Like

David, Jim was also gay. So was Bruce. The only difference was that Bruce didn't want anyone to know that he was gay because of his job. He was about my age and lived in Virginia with his life partner. His partner also had to hide his orientation because he was in the commercial mortgage industry. On some occasions I'd have "business" type dates with Bruce so he could play the straight role in front of his peers and he gave me design work in return.

But he was right, I had to decide about what I was going to do. I had to get a life back. I pondered my quandary for days, going over all of the pros and cons. I wanted my life back but I was scared. My face was still puffy on both sides of my mouth where I had been knifed. My appearance didn't bother me as much as the awful feeling of apprehension that loomed before me...my attacker was still loose and I could identify him. Would he come after me and kill me in order to save himself?

I decided to go back. Bruce said that he wanted me to stay at his house in Virginia. "You can stay with me and Irv for as long as you like...until you get your own place." It was an open invitation to stay, with a post script that I also had to leave. That was okay because I didn't want to stay there indefinitely. My plan was to live with them while I finished the Riggs Bank material and also find my own place in time to get my daughter into school.

We drove to Virginia on a Sunday early in August. I went on the weekend because I wanted Bruce and Irv to be there when I arrived. He had offered to leave a key hidden for me so I could arrive at any time but I said no, I'd be there by 5 p.m. I didn't tell Bruce, but I had a real problem going into an empty house. When that situation presented itself, I had to check every room and even behind the shower curtain before closing the front door. I knew I was being totally paranoid but it became a psychotic ritual—the way some people constantly wash their hands.

Bruce and Irv owned a handsome home in Northern Virginia about 18 miles from Washington, D.C. It was an easy commute because they were within a mile of the local metro stop.

The entire house was carpeted with a relaxing plush, pale-blue rug. There was a spacious den with a fireplace and a TV in the basement. This was Irv's nesting place. Bruce liked to be on the main floor, with the pastel paintings in the living room, the blond mahogany dining room, and the tiled gourmet kitchen. Upstairs, he gave us the guest room to share. It had two twin beds and a guest bathroom across the hall. Bruce and Irv shared the master bedroom which had its own luxurious spa-type bath.

I was satisfied with the arrangement. They even helped me set-up a mini-office in the kitchen. So everything seemed okay until Monday. On Monday, Bruce and Irving left together at about 8 a.m. I started to make a list of the things I needed to do in order to create the Bank's brochure. I had started to work on it in May but what I had done was put in storage. It seemed easier to just start all over again. First I would make a layout and conceptualize the format. Then I would write the copy and do the camera-ready-art. After Bruce approved of everything, I would bid the job out to a few printers. In all, I guessed it would take about 2-3 weeks.

As I was sitting there doing my plans, I heard some sort of noise outside. My daughter was sitting in the kitchen with me. I freaked out. I thought of calling the police or maybe peeking out of the windows. "Shhh!" I said to my daughter, then I signaled to her to sit on the floor and I did, too. We hid behind the kitchen counter so if anyone looked in the windows they couldn't see us. We stayed like that, on the floor, for maybe an hour. It had been quiet: no more unexplained noises. I whispered, "O.K., we're gonna just walk around and check the house." I took her hand and we slowly got up. Then we tip-toed throughout the home checking every room and every closet. From the top floor we glanced out of the windows. It was a sunny, warm day with no one around. "Okay, we're going to do some errands and have lunch."

The whole month went like that. I'd work in the kitchen or go out to get things. When I came back I'd check the whole house to make sure there was no one there. I had many false alarms like that first one on Monday. But I was getting the job done and also worrying about where I was going to live. I was zeroing in on a city in Maryland where I had a couple of business friends. It was about 75 miles away from the city where I had been knifed. I started buying the paper to check-out the Real Estate sections.

Finally, the job for Bruce was done. My daughter would have to start school in less than a couple of weeks, so I had to act fast. I made an appointment to see an apartment that seemed to fit my needs. It was a long drive from Virginia. When I got there I liked what I saw. The manager showed me the only two bedroom unit that was available. It was very attractive. It was on the first floor and faced the outdoor swimming pool. I was uncomfortable with being on the first floor for safety reasons and I told the manager that I had recently been the victim of a crime. "Can I put my own lock on the front door, with my own key?" "Sure, I can't see why not", she said. So I took the apartment.

We were able to move in about a week later. At last, I was able to get my things out of storage. Then I hurried to get my daughter registered into school.

On the first evening there, I just sat up all night. The second night I slept one hour sitting-up, and so it went for the first year.

On the third day someone was banging on my sliding glass door. I froze for a moment and then inched my way towards the door. I peeked out. Standing outside was a grayish-white haired guy in shorts and a tee-shirt. He didn't have any shoes on. In one hand he held two books and in the other, a bottle of wine. When he saw me peeking out, he yelled, "Hey! I'm your neighbor" pointing to where he lived. "I brought you some welcoming gifts..."

I wasn't sure of what to do. I had a Charlie Bar installed on the sliding glass door and didn't want to open it. I indicated for him to go around to the front door. When he got there, I opened the door and there stood a prematurely gray, blue-eyed Irishman who seemed to be a little tipsy. He held up two books. "I've brought you my two favorite books: *The Joy of Cooking* and *The Joy of Sex*, and a good bottle to drink while you're doing either one." He made me feel at ease immediately and I invited him in. We sat in the kitchen drinking the wine and getting to know each other.

My new friend was Jim, the nephew of a famous movie star. He was originally from Connecticut and had lived in Maryland for at least twenty years. Jim was divorced with two kids but didn't want to talk about it. He was about six or seven years older than me and worked for a well-established construction company. He was their Marketing Director and so he wore a suit and tie rather than a hard hat and jeans. I could see that he apparently drank a lot but I didn't feel that it was my place to judge his lifestyle. After a couple of hours he left and on his way out suggested that I meet him at a popular watering hole/restaurant the following night—at happy hour. He said he would introduce me to everyone that I needed to know in this town.

IX. COMING OUT

I was beginning to feel that there was "safety in numbers" here and the next night proved that to be true. I met Jim at the bar and there were about 30 people there. He introduced me to about 20 of them and they were all very gracious. I stayed friends with all of them for the next two and a half years.

I wound up having a brief affair with Jim. Brief because of his excessive drinking. The alcoholism made him undependable and impotent. We did a lot of inspiring things together, though. He took me sailing on his friend's sailboat. This friend of his, Kevin, was known as "the old man and the sea". He was a short, white-haired, plump Irish elf with laughing blue eyes and a wry sense of humor. His 24 foot Catalina, the "Miss Mary", was the love of his life. The second love of his life was Mary, his wife. The two of them were hilarious. They were in their early seventies and retired from life in Washington, D.C. Mary wouldn't go sailing with him because she had skin cancer so he would always invite a couple of people to go with him. The rule was: if you wanted to sail with Kevin, you have to bring lunch; preferably egg salad sandwiches. No booze while at sea but you could drink all you wanted to at the dock or in the bar, which Kevin and Jim did. I remained good friends with Kevin and Mary for many years and was asked to deliver the eulogy at his funeral 20 years later.

Jim and I didn't actually break-up because there was nothing really to break-up. We were unsuccessful lovers who were friendly. That was good because in October I met Bob. He bought me a drink at the bar and we chatted for awhile. He was a Captain with United Airlines. He had recently moved there from Cape Hatteras, S.C. Of course, he was divorced, as were about 90 percent of this crowd. He had a daughter about my daughter's age but he was 20 years older than me. I wasn't romantically interested in him and he seemed to be hooked with a local real estate lady by the name of Lynn.

I was quite surprised when he called me. Bob was a pleasant guy. We chatted for a few minutes and then he said he had a book for me—one that he thought I'd enjoy, could he drop it off at my place? It was about 4 in the afternoon. I was at home working and he was on his "off" schedule which meant he flew for three days and then had four days off.

Sure, why not, I thought. He lived only a half a mile away and within a few minutes he was at my door. He was tall, maybe 6'3" or so with fair skin and fair hair with gray creeping into the sides. His blue eyes seemed enormous because of the thick glasses that he wore. Then I noticed he also wore hearing aids in both ears. I wondered how he was able to physically qualify as a Captain for United Airlines. Apparently these handicaps did not interfere with his abilities. He later explained to me that "it doesn't make any difference...everything is computerized."

He handed me the book: *Illusions*, by Richard Bach. I had mentioned to him that I both wrote and read poetry. He said that although this book wasn't poetry—it was good prose and he thought that I would enjoy it. I did enjoy it but it was not Y Garcia Lorca or Danté material, and it was a bit mundane. But that's okay, it was a nice thought plus there aren't too many men who read Danté for pleasure as I did.

These men, in this town, seemed to think I needed books; first Jim, now Bob...my thoughts were interrupted by the phone ringing.

"Is Bob there?" "Excuse me?" "Can I talk to Bob?" Somewhat baffled, I handed the phone to Bob. I tried not to listen. Bob sounded annoyed. "I'll call *you* later..." and he hung up. I didn't ask him who it was but I *did* want to know how that person got my phone number. Bob had my number because I had given him one of my cards when I had met him.

"That was Lynn. She's a little possessive sometimes. Your number? I suspect that she may have gone through my wallet and copied your number off of your card—*I* didn't give it to her."

I didn't need this kind of crap in my life. An old, soon-to-retire pilot and his jealous mistress...she might be nuttier than the guy who attacked me. I told Bob how I felt (but not about the old retired pilot part).

He said he wanted to be friends and that he resented Lynn for interfering with that. I kind of agreed with his reasoning, but I still felt her to be a threat.

"How bout if we have brunch on Saturday? I know a nice little place downtown that makes Eggs Benedict and Bloody Mary's on Saturdays."

He was right, it *was* a nice little place with dark wood paneling and round pine tables draped with red checkered linens. I thoroughly enjoyed the poached eggs nesting atop crisp Canadian bacon on a muffin. The potatoes along side had been sauteed with bacon and shallots. "Haven't you eaten lately?" Bob inquired. "What do you mean?" "I mean you ate everything except the silver and china." I laughed, "It was very good!" "Well, then, let's do this every Saturday if I'm in town. I have to work next Saturday. Going to Chicago, then a layover in San Francisco, back to Chicago and home Monday night."

Eventually Bob and I became lovers. The "older man" thing kind of intrigued me. It almost felt naughty, as though I was sleeping with my father.

When he broke up with Lynn she called me...and she called me every name in the book... "You fucking whore, you knew Bob was my boyfriend. I saw you chasing him all over town...you fucking whore..." I kept hanging up on her. Finally, I called Bob and told him about it. She had been calling me non-stop, night and day, every day. She was hysterical. I had only met her twice. She was attractive. She had coiffed strawberry blond hair surrounding a somewhat chubby face. She was short and very aggressive like Harriet and Nancy. But Lynn was in her late fifties And there lay the problem; the root of her ferocious jealousy: she didn't have the time that I had. We were on different clocks.

Bob said that he would take care of it and he did. I never heard from her after that and I never saw her. The town's little grapevine suggested that she had actually moved away.

Our relationship was really a lot of fun. He had a 14 foot Hobi Cat that we went out on a lot and we went bike riding and out to dinner. On several occasions we got our girls together and they hit it off, too.

There was a routine established. On his days off, if it was during the week, we'd go out to lunch and back to his place for what's affectionally known as a "nooner". This worked out well because it was while my daughter was in school. Then, sometimes I'd get a sitter and go over to his place in the evening and he'd make dinner. This was a treat for me. He'd usually make the same thing but it was good: he'd make a broiled steak lathered with bar-b-que sauce, a micro waved baked potato and canned corn or frozen broccoli.

His apartment was really nice. It was actually a water-front condo that he was renting. It was a two bedroom unit. He used the smaller bedroom as a bedroom/office. It was where his daughter, Amber, stayed when she visited him. There was a cozy fireplace in the living room and next to it he kept a large glass rifle case which held about twenty carefully cleaned and oiled guns. One of his hobbies was duck hunting. The guns didn't bother me. In fact, I felt safer with arms-at-hand, like I did when I was carrying Warren's unloaded Luger.

During one of our afternoon trysts we had a peculiar, almost harrowing but at the same time, hilarious event. We were on his bed making mad passionate love. It is important to note the placement of the bed: the headboard was against the wall. The bed was not centered in the room. It had about a one foot space from the wall on the left and about a ten foot space from the wall on the right, so naturally, you got into the bed on the right side.

In our moment of passion we somehow rolled off of the left side of the bed. There we were—our legs entwined while we were firmly embedded in the one foot space between the wall and bed. We were stuck there. We couldn't figure out how to get un-stuck. We couldn't reach the phone—to call who? The fire department? I don't think so.

We were stuck there like that for at least a half an hour. Bob was a big guy and I was tall, too, so maneuvering without breaking an arm or a leg was very tricky. Somehow, we became miraculously disengaged. It sounds like a bad joke, but it actually was a little scary. We had pondered the circumstances and fantasized about having a rescue squad cut an escape hole in the wall that trapped us.

Afterwards, we laughed about it, and Bob, who was in the "macho" mind set, even bragged about it to a few of his pilot buddies.

Our fun continued for a year. We did lots of adventurous things like trying to sail on a fifty-mile trip in August; sail on his *Hobi-Cat*. Generally, there's no wind in August and being a "Captain" he should have known that. Well, we got stuck about 25 miles from shore in a dead calm and he didn't know what to do. We sat on the trampoline of the boat, in 90° weather for over an hour. He kept saying that someone would find us and tow us in. Since his plan wasn't working, I finally took out my compact from my purse and signaled to a boat with my mirror. That boat came and towed us in and Bob was genuinely both grateful and embarrassed by the whole event.

My business was doing fairly well in this new town. I had met a lot of people and at that time in my career, my portfolio held many notable examples. I had all the promotional work that I had created for the new Taubman Mall, and that mall became very well known throughout the Metro area. It was noted because of Taubman's innovations—his use of glass elevators and performing arts arenas. I was able to show my work for Riggs Bank and the Holiday Inn, plus a handful of other accounts. I also had "dubs" of radio spots that I had produced, including the famous one with Ravel's "Bolero"—famous because it aired on a Washington, D.C. FM station and everybody talked about it. (That was good). I also had a couple of bi-lines: columns that I wrote for local magazines and newspapers. At that point in my life, my daughter called me "Motor Mom". I also penned promotional work for Ken Burns when he was producing the "Civil War" series for the Corporation for Public Broadcasting.

I was glad to be back in my groove. The gruesome attack was behind me now and I was reinventing myself. I was able to get a few local accounts: a hotel and promo work for a radio station, but most of the work was from D.C. It was a long drive, much further away from where I used to live but I wanted the types of accounts that only the District could generate. So I made the trip into town a couple of times a week.

Towards the end of 1981, I got a peculiar call one morning. It was on a day that I was working at home. It was Joe. Joe was one of the 15 or so divorced guys in our crowd. I had talked to him a few times and had run into him at private parties. He was going with Chrissy, a forty-something stewardess. The group of us, besides meeting at the one bar for happy hour, also patronized a local coffee shop in the morning. To locals, it was simply referred to as "The Delly". (As in: The Farmer in the *Dell*) . "Can you meet me at the Delly? It's very important. I've got to talk to you." Joe sounded grave. It was about 8:30 a.m. and I thought that maybe he had some business for me. Joe ran his own company. He basically sold quality gold jewelry and gold bricks, as well. He did trade shows, displaying his wares all over the country to jewelers or anyone else who was interested. I had vaguely talked to him about doing a brochure that he could hand-out at the shows, telling him that it would look really classy if it was gold embossed.

So, I went to the Delly. It was about halfway between my apartment and Bob's condo. It was a small place—maybe only eight tables. When I walked in, I observed that Joe looked very sullen. That wasn't his usual style. He was generally upbeat with a whacky sense of humor. He was a tall, good looking guy with almost-black hair. I guessed that he was maybe fifty. He dressed pretty well and always wore a huge chunky gold pinkie ring on each hand, plus several strands of gold chains around his neck. That morning he had on a black turtleneck with a tan blazer with black slacks.

I sat down at his table, very curious about what he *had* to tell me. "You want some coffee?" he asked while signaling the waitress. "Sure."

I was not prepared for what he was about to tell me. His girlfriend, Chrissy, had somewhat of a reputation for being "loose", I had even heard that she was a nympho, but I never paid attention to gossip. I knew Chrissy to say "Hi" and that was about it.

Joe told me that he suspected Chrissy had been cheating on him so he began to follow her. He said he followed her to Bob's apartment last week. "No!" I remarked, laughing. It was like a bad joke. "Yes!"

"She walked up to his door, last Wednesday night around one a.m." "No." I repeated. "Before she rang the bell she took her sweater and bra off and stood there naked from the waist-up." "What?!" "Yeah, and then he answered the door and they started kissing and then she went inside. She stayed till almost three in the morning."

I was having a hard time digesting this, but unfortunately, I could picture the scenario, especially with her reputation. Chrissy was an overly-made-up bleached blond forty-year-old who worked part-time as a stewardess. The rest of the time she was usually drunk and always had this ridiculous grin on her face, even at funerals. She was divorced from a pilot and I knew that the ex was an acquaintance of Bob's. So I guessed that it sorta could be true.

"But that's not all. I was parked outside of her house last night and who showed up? — Bob. So, listen to what I did: I called the fire department and said that the house was on fire. When they arrived with their sirens blaring, Bob and Chrissy came running out of the house naked as blue jays." "Oh, my *God*." "I photographed it." "What?" "Yeah, and here's a copy for you.:"

I was stunned, absolutely stunned. I didn't know what to do. All I knew was that I had to get away from Joe. Just get away and think. I thanked him for the information and looking at my watch, told him that I had to go meet a client. I was out of there.

When I got home I took the picture out of my purse. I thought about our relationship. It had been good and I cared about Bob. At that point he had been building a house on a little piece of waterfront property that he had purchased. He had been implying that he wanted me to live with him there and sought my opinion as he was designing the blueprints. He said he was building an artist's studio in the loft and it had a spectacular view of the cove where his land was situated. I had told Bob that I wanted to get back to painting some day.

I had studied painting with Sidney Tillem and Margaret Beck, both renowned New York artists. They were professors at Parsons and I had taken a minor in fine art. While working at Macy's, I painted quite a lot. I even did a couple of shows: one out in the Hamptons at a gallery that Willem DeKooning showed at regularly, and a show in New York at the Francis X. Callahan Gallery. I actually did fairly well at both shows. Bob was a pretty good artist himself and so I knew that he could appreciate my talent. The fact that he was designing his own house didn't surprise me at all because I knew he was capable of doing it.

We had a great deal in common and it was a comfortable relationship. And so I was somewhat humiliated by what Joe had told me. I decided to meet with Bob and ask him about it before I made any rash decisions.

I called him at about 11:00 a.m. that same morning. He was at home. He had mentioned to me the previous day that he was leaving that night around 9:00 p.m. for a three-day flight plan and usually he didn't go out the day before he was flying. "Hey! Are you free for brunch?" I was trying to sound cheery. "There's something important that I need to ask you about." "Well, o.k., Hon, but I can't drink anything—I'm flying tonight." "That's o.k. I'm not that crazy about drinking in the daytime—you know that." "How about 12:30?" "That'll be good, Bob. I'll see you at *our* brunch bar!"

We had become regulars at the first restaurant he had taken me to for brunch. We even had our own special table in the back, by the fireplace.

We hooked-up in the vestibule of the restaurant and were seated in the back at our table. "So, what's up?" he wanted to get right to the point. "Let's order first." We had our usual Eggs Benedict and coffee instead of Bloody Marys. I was still quiet. When the eggs arrived, I delicately punctured the gold yolks and watched the rich ochre-colored liquid travel down the sides of Canadian Bacon and get absorbed into the muffin. Bob was being patient. "Joe called me this morning." "Oh, yeah?" What did *he* want?" "I met him for coffee at the Delly." There was a gap of silence, whether Bob suspected that I knew about the affair or not was hard to tell. "He wanted to discuss you and Chrissy. He was pretty upset." Another silence, an uncomfortable hanging moment whereupon *he* knew that *I* knew. "What did he tell you?" "He told me *everything*." I was beginning to lose my cool. I reached into my bag and pulled out the photo and put it on the table, actually threw it onto the table.

So then Bob began a narrative about how he had known Chrissy for twenty years and how he was just doing her a favor, blah, blah, blah.

"Oh, bullshit!" I blurted out. Defensively, he pointed out that we had no formal ties, that I shouldn't feel so threatened. "Well, what about Joe? Don't you think you were sort of interfering with his relationship?" I could see that there would be no resolution to the conversation. I had been burnt and after my ex-husband's philandering, I had made the decision not to ever go through it again. How could I ever trust Bob? We finished our brunch in silence and I noted a very pained expression on his face—in his eyes. I suspected he had been through this before and that having several women was his lifestyle. It had taken me a year to figure *that* one out.

We parted on a very cool note, with no mention of the future, nothing about, "I'll call you when I get back." And he *didn't* call me when he got back. I think he was waiting for me to call him. But I didn't. I couldn't. As much as I cared for him, I made the decision that I just didn't want that kind of relationship. I saw him around town a couple of times after that. He was alone and looking very sad, and I was tempted to give-in, but I just couldn't.

Then, a couple of months later I saw him out with Jan. Jan! of *all* people. I never liked Jan. She was about 10 years older than me and had been having an affair with a married man who had died of cancer. She even had the nerve to go to this man's wake whereupon the man's wife literally threw her out of the funeral parlor. She was tall and very mannish. Jan wore her gray hair short, trimmed like a young boy. She didn't wear any make-up and was not what you'd call glamorous. She worked as a secretary. From the few times I had chatted with her I was able to ascertain that she was divorced and had two teenage boys who lived with their father. Her skin was always tan and I later learned that it wasn't from the sun: it was from her ethnic background. Apparently she was of Spanish descent.

I was very surprised one afternoon when Jan called me. We weren't "calling" friends. We really weren't more than acquaintances. "What's up?" I asked her. "I wanted to know if you were planning on going back with Bob?" I was taken aback—what kind of question was that? "And *why* is that any of *your* business?" "Well, I didn't want to interfere..." "Well, then, *don't*!" And I hung up on her. The nerve of that bitch!

After that they were seen all over town together and I thought to myself, "good-riddens". About six months later, when Bob finished his dream house, I heard that she had moved in with him. This was a *very* small town.

I was still friends with my neighbor, Jim, and continued to go sailing with him and Kevin on the "Miss Mary" until I got a very compelling phone call.

X. A WITNESS FOR THE PROSECUTION

It was towards the end of winter, 1982. "How did you find me?"

"I'm a detective, I'm supposed to find people." This was the call I had been dreading. The whole thing flashed through my mind: The force of the sweaty hands on my mouth, the struggle, the feel of the knife slashing across my cheeks. I could almost feel the oozing, warm, blood dripping down the sides of my face and the humiliation of taking my clothes off. I felt both frozen and vulnerable at the same time.

I lit a cigarette and quickly inhaled, for some reason expecting to inhale blood. I choked on the cigarette and muttered, "What is it?" "We have a suspect. I realize it's been a long time, almost two years...but I was wondering if you would be willing to look at some photographs..." "I don't know. You can't tell anyone where I live, *please*, no one must know...he's gonna come after me." "I assure you, the suspect does not know where you are, he doesn't even know that I've contacted you. It's very important that you try to identify him so we can lock him up. Don't you want him locked up?" "Of course I do!" "Detective Neville and the State Prosecutor will be there with me. So is there some place you can meet us? Oh, and I want you to bring your daughter along, she's a witness to the crime."

I wasn't sure of what to do. I wanted the guy locked up, but at the same time I was afraid of the process. For almost two years I had been hiding in another area of the state. I had endeavored to get my life back. I lived everyday looking over my shoulder, aware of my surroundings, having an unlisted phone number. I still had problems sleeping.

"I don't know, Detective Williams. Can I call you back? Would you give me your phone number and I'll call you back?"

"Sure." He gave me his number and I promised to get back to

him the next day. He had said that time was of the essence and I understood his urgency, it's just that I had to feel comfortable with the procedure. I had to digest this sudden turn in my life and weigh the dangers involved. I was also worried about my daughter. She was now ten years old. The attack had been very traumatic for her but she seemed to have adjusted well. She had a lot of new friends where we were and I think she felt secure. I decided to be frank with her about it and see how she felt about looking at the photos.

I hadn't expected the detectives to find the perpetrator after so long and my daughter and I never talked about it, so when I told her that the detective had called me she was very surprised. She was a lot stronger than I had imagined—even more assertive than me. She said she definitely wanted to meet with the detectives to look at photographs, that she'd be *glad* to.

Okay, I thought, I guess we're going to do this. I had no idea where this was leading to; I had no experience as a crime "witness". My reasoning skills regarding the attack were still somewhat muddled because I was still suffering from some sort of trauma as a result of the event. I knew that the detectives knew where I lived and yet I refused to meet them in that city. In my irrational mind I thought that the suspect would follow Williams and Neville and find out where I lived. This is how victims of crime think, so when I called Detective Williams back, I told him that we could meet at a Marriott Hotel located next to the Washington Beltway, about fifty miles from my home.

Apparently he was willing to meet me anywhere. We all gathered there a few days later: Detectives Williams and Neville, along with the State Prosecutor, Anne Harrington. My daughter and me got there first and I went into the restaurant and asked for the smoking section. If they needed me as a witness, they were going to have to let me smoke.

They arrived shortly after us. Williams introduced me to Ms. Harrington. We chatted informally for a few minutes and then Ms. Harrington explained to me what her role would be if there was a trial. "I will use every conceivable law at my disposal to convict him. I will gather an abundance of evidence, including your testimony and your daughter's testimony, to get him locked up...get him put away for a long time. In most of these types of cases, the prosecutor usually wins. We won't go to trial unless we're 99% sure of our success."

She was very convincing. I also felt at ease with her. She was outgoing and friendly and very determined to see justice served. The detectives then asked who wanted to look at photos first? Me or my daughter? We had to look separately so that the identification process wasn't coerced.

I went first while Ms. Harrington took my daughter outside. I looked at the six photos for a long time. A queasy feeling started to come over me. He was there and I pointed at the photo in the left of the center. That was him. Looking at him made me very uncomfortable. The fear was climbing up my back and I looked around the restaurant to make sure he wasn't there in person.

"Let me go get my daughter..." I had to get out of there, away from that photograph. I brought my daughter back and this time Ms. Harrington stayed at the table while I waited in the lobby. I was only there maybe ten minutes when they all came out of the restaurant. "Okay, we've got what we want. We'll be in touch with you," Williams said. "How did we do? Was that the guy?" "We really can't tell you that, but I'd say you did good. Thanks for meeting with us."

Ms. Harrington indicated that she would like to talk to me at length in a few days. "Can you come to my office? I really need to meet with you in my office next time." "Well, I guess so, if I *have* to."

We left it at that. We quickly went to my car and I started to drive home. On the way, my mind was eddying in emotion. I was having flashbacks of the crime but also pondering what the future might entail. The detectives had mentioned that we might have to go to a "line-up" to identify the man. We might wind-up in Court testifying. And I worried about this guy coming after me again. I decided that I should talk to an attorney.

I had met Sol Rosen socially on several occasions in Washington. Sol became renown when he was representing Bernard Welsh, the jewel thief in McLean, Virginia, who killed Dr. Halberstam. In that particular case, Welsh wound-up firing Rosen as his public defender because Rosen was trying to secure a book deal on the case. Welsh said the book rights belonged to *him* and he fired Rosen. Even though Sol was known for defending criminals, I figured that he could look at both sides of the fence and made an appointment with him in his D.C. office.

The second floor office which was located a few blocks off North Capitol Street, had walls that were literally plastered with yellowed newspaper articles. Sol had a way of getting into the news and not always favorably.

He was a fiftyish, balding, bespeckled, plump bachelor. His Brooklyn accent was guttural and thick, and he was quick to spout-out questions while thoughtfully listening to answers.

"So what's going on? You ever go to Club Elan anymore?" "No, Sol, I live too far away." Sol hung out at the local clubs and discos around town. He usually had one glass of wine or a coke and munched on the happy hour freebies. He wasn't much of a spender, although I do remember that he bought me a drink once.

I began my long saga about the attempted murder and how I had survived the last two years. I told him about meeting with Neville, Williams and Harrington, and the prospect of going to a line-up and a hearing. He listened very intently. "I can't help you."

"Honestly, I'd like to, but I'm gonna have you call someone else, a friend of mine, up in Montgomery County. He's very good—I've known him for years. Just call the guy, and tell him I sent you. You'll be okay."

I didn't feel like I accomplished anything by meeting with him, other than two friends having a chat. But I decided that I would call his friend: Thomas Fortune Faye. I liked his name, anyway.

A few days later Detective Williams called me. It was now towards the end of March. They were getting a line-up ready and he needed me and my daughter to go to the detention center as soon as possible. This was located at least 75 miles from where I lived and I explained that I would have to miss work and that my daughter would have to miss school. He then mentioned that if and when I testified at a hearing, I'd be reimbursed for my expenses because I'd be a witness for the State. That was news to me. I really had no idea how these things worked.

The prospect of looking at this creep through a glass window terrified me. Again, my logic was escaping me and I was allowing fear to purge my emotions.

We agreed to a day and time. I carefully explained to my daughter what we had to do. She didn't appear to be terribly daunted by the procedure. She just said, "Okay, Mom." The detective assured me that he'd be there, too.

When we arrived we were escorted down a cinder-block hallway to a door with a small glass panel. I was told to look in the window and state if I recognized anyone. "Oh, God! He can see me!" I whispered as I ducked below the window. "No, he can't." the attending officer said. I was *sure* that he *could*. He had looked straight at me. "Ma'am, he can't see you, really. That's a one-way glass. Please get up so we can continue." I was shaking. I stood up and looked in the window again. "I recognize number four." "And how do you recognize that man?" "He's the guy who tried to kill me almost two years ago...in my apartment." "Okay, good. Would you have your daughter step up here please?"

It was over in ten minutes. That *was* the guy. My nerves were rattled and I was terrified. I had to get out of there. I grabbed my daughter's hand and quickly led her out to the car. On my way home I started to wonder if I really wanted to get involved in this thing, if I wanted my life turned upside-down again. It was not an easy decision, one that I would ponder for days. I still had to meet with Ms. Harrington before I made my decision, and with Tom Faye.

I was able to get an appointment with Tom right away. Sol Rosen had called him, and he was expecting my call. He agreed to meet me at the same Marriott that the detectives and prosecutor had met me at because his office was also about 75 miles away from where I lived.

Tom was an easy-going guy. Like Sol, he was middle-aged and a little plump. He seemed like a caring kind of guy and listened intently as I laid the cards on the table. I was getting used to telling and re-telling the sordid details of the attempted murder, in fact, I told it unemotionally as though I was reading a newspaper.

I didn't expect his response. How could I? I had absolutely no experience as a witness for the prosecution. "This is the way it goes: I will attend the trial, and I'm pretty sure there's gonna be a trial, and then we'll see what happens. Either way, there's a lawsuit here—there's a *big* lawsuit.

"Oh, no, I meant, I mean I'm not planning on suing—I just thought I might need a lawyer for some reason."

"You've got to sue; and here's how you do it—if he's convicted, great, our case is won. If he goes free, we file a civil suit."

Suddenly I was gripped with fear. "What do you mean, if he goes free? Anne Harrington said she has a 99% shot at getting him convicted."

"It would be a jury trial and in a jury trial, it's something that you can't predict. Anyway, why don't we start with this: I'll be present at the trial, pro bono—free-of-charge. After we hear the verdict we can discuss how you want to proceed. Now, I'm going to go with the understanding that you're going to retain my services at the end of the trial."

"Okay."

I didn't really know what I was getting into. I still had to meet with the prosecutor and see what she had to say.

That night, I called my neighbor, Jim. When I had first met him,—the day he brought over the books and the wine, I had told him about the attempt on my life.

He had been very understanding and comforting and he said, "If you ever need any help with that, let me know." Well, I needed some help. I was getting really wound-up about what had developed. I asked him if he could come over to my place—that I needed to talk to him about something, and he cheerfully said "Sure!"

This time he was carrying a bottle of Vodka, but no books. It was about 8:30 p.m. and my daughter was already asleep. Jim was a little tipsy, but lucid enough to hear me out. I told him about how they had nabbed a suspect and how we had gone to the line-up. "I'm afraid that there's going to be a jury trial, and I'm going to *have* to testify, and my daughter will have to testify, too."

"I'll go with you." It was what I was hoping to hear, I guess. I wasn't going to ask him, so when he volunteered, I jumped on it. "That'll be great. I really appreciate it."

Jim hadn't been working that much lately and apparently, he had no problem taking time off from his job. So it was all set—if my daughter and me had to testify—he'd be there for moral support. He even suggested that he go along with me when I had to meet with the prosecutor which was going to be in a few days.

His support, the emotional support, helped me a great deal. So I began to focus on what had to be done—the meetings and pre-trial preparations that lay ahead, and the great hope that there would finally be justice, that there would be a conviction: that this maniac would be locked-up and I would be free.

The trial was scheduled for the first week in April, 1982.

Z at age four.

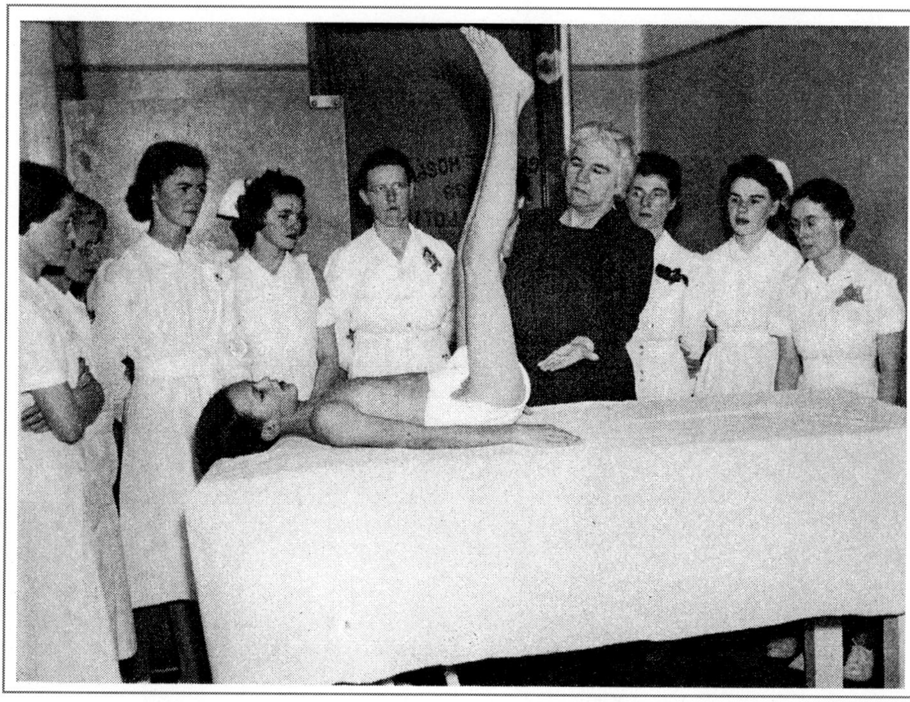

Sister Kenny demonstrating her
polio treatment.

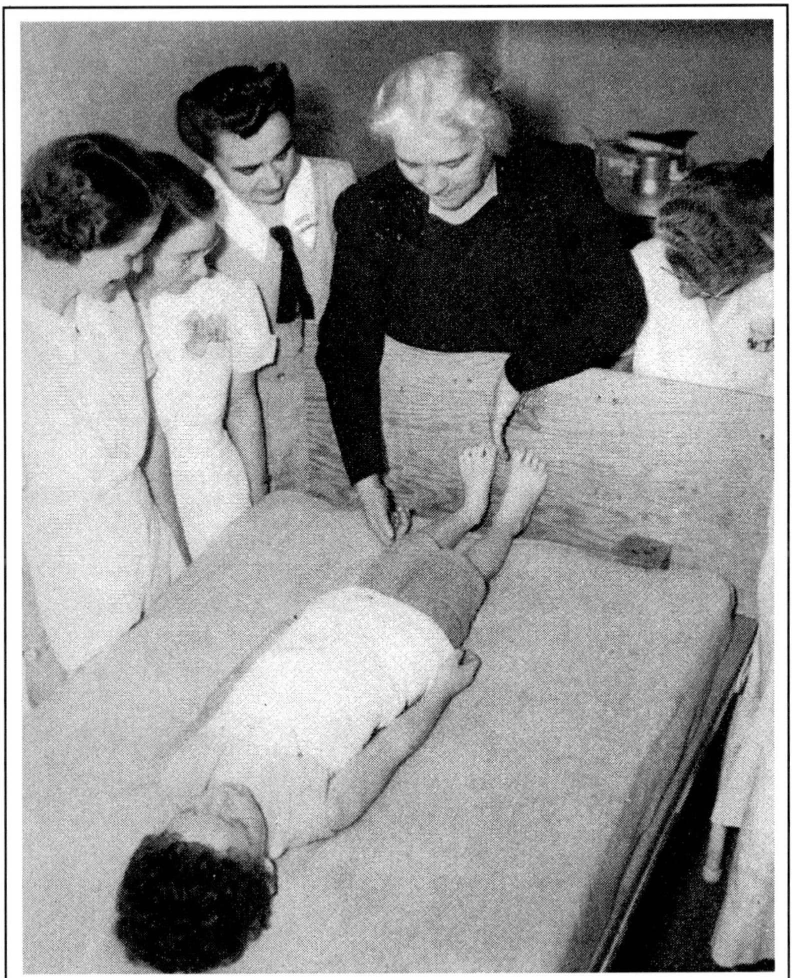

Sister Kenny training nurses in her method.

Professor and Artist Rosemarie Beck: one of
Z's Mentors at Parsons School of Design, N.Y.

U.S.S. Joseph P. Kennedy, Jr. (DD 850)

Dining critic, "Commandor Whitehead" and Z at
A restaurant in Washington, D.C.

Z with Duke at Duke Zeibert's Restaurant,

Washington, D.

Z with Peter Graves at Duke Zeibert's.

John Ritter and Jon Voight with Z at a
Private Function in Washington, D.C.

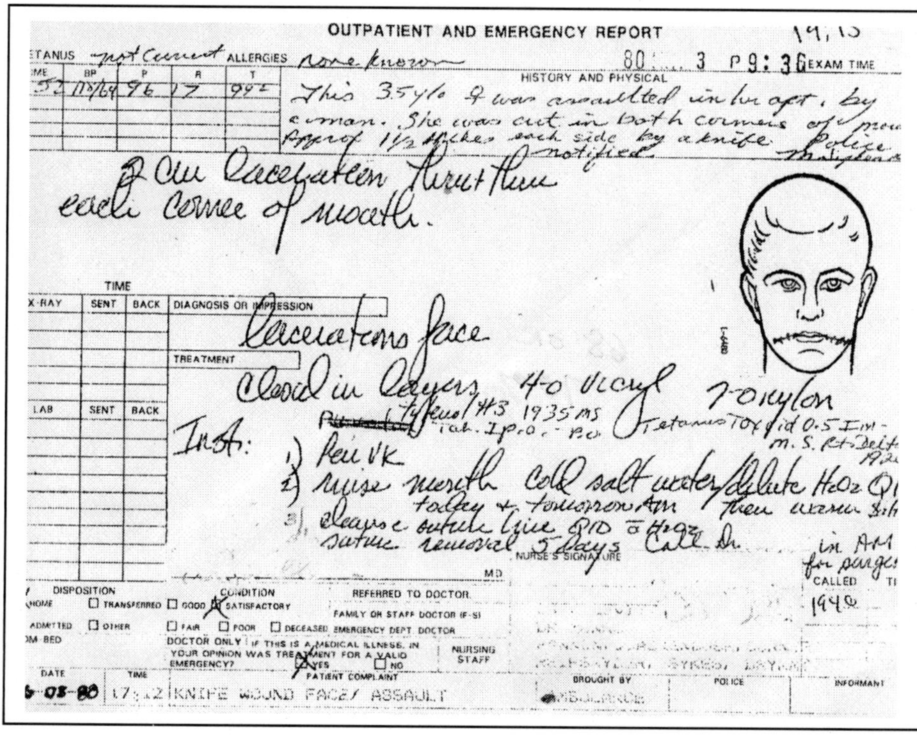

OUTPATIENT AND EMERGENCY REPORT

TETANUS not current ALLERGIES none known

HISTORY AND PHYSICAL

This 35 y/o ♀ was assaulted in her apt. by a man. She was cut in both corners of mouth approx 1½ inches each side by a knife. Police notified.

DIAGNOSIS OR IMPRESSION

Lacerations face

TREATMENT

Closed in layers 4-0 vicryl 7-0 nylon

Tetanus toxoid 0.5 IM

Inst:

1) Pen VK

2) rinse mouth cold salt water/dilute H_2O_2 today + tomorrow AM then warm salt

3) cleanse outside line QID c̄ H_2O_2 suture removal 5 days Call Dr. in AM for surgeon

NURSE'S SIGNATURE

DISPOSITION: HOME / TRANSFERRED / ADMITTED / OTHER

CONDITION: GOOD / SATISFACTORY (X) / FAIR / POOR / DECEASED

REFERRED TO DOCTOR: FAMILY OR STAFF DOCTOR (F-S) / EMERGENCY DEPT. DOCTOR

DOCTOR ONLY: IF THIS IS A MEDICAL ILLNESS, IN YOUR OPINION WAS TREATMENT FOR A VALID EMERGENCY? YES (X) NO

CALLED 1940

DATE 5-03-80 TIME 17:12 PATIENT COMPLAINT KNIFE WOUND FACE/ ASSAULT

BROUGHT BY AMBULANCE POLICE INFORMANT

Emergency Room report illustrating Z's knife wound.

Dear Mommy,
I Love you very
much. I hope one
of these things
never happens
agin.

Letter to Z from daughter, June 3, 1980.

XI. THE TRIAL

I was scheduled to meet with Anne Harrington a few days before the trial began. I took Jim up on his offer and he came along with me. Thank God he was sober. I was beginning to think that his participation: as an ally, was good therapy for him. He was an alcoholic and by helping me he was helping himself—he was forcing himself into sobriety, at least during the day.

Anne was very impressive as a person, and as a prosecutor. She was a small, attractive woman with dark hair and intense brown eyes. I judged her age to be in the late thirties to early forties. She was articulate and precise. I was at ease with her and felt a certain confidence in her objective to get my attacker convicted. After about an hour, our meeting finally ended. We had discussed the questions that she would be asking me and my daughter and warned me that the defense attorney might get rough on me, even though I was the victim. I had heard that often occurs in rape trials, where the victim is actually accused of allegedly leading the rapist on—of abetting the crime. That is what had happened to me during the pre-trial hearing with the U.S. Navy regarding the accident aboard the U.S.S. Kennedy. They had asked me some very intimidating questions and had tried to humiliate me even though *I* was the one who fell overboard because *they* hadn't secured the lifeline.

We all shook hands. Our next meeting would take place in Montgomery County, Maryland in the Circuit Court on April 5, 1982.

Since we were driving about 70 miles during rush hour, we decided to leave at 7:30 a.m. Jim came by to get us around 7:10 a.m. We were going in his car which was good because I was so nervous that I probably wouldn't have managed very well. My daughter was fine, she wasn't troubled at all. I, on the other was *so* scared at the prospect of being in the same room as the offender: being face-to-face with him, that I wore a hat to hide my hair and also wore a pair of sunglasses to help hide my identity. Later, the defense attorney would make disparaging remarks about my costume.

We got there just in time. The courtroom was filling up. Tom Faye was there. The two detectives, Williams and Neville, were there. The *defendant* was there. I was the first one being called to testify as the primary witness for the State. I was sworn in and it began.

In the following documentary, the defendant is referred to as “X”, my daughter is known as “Y”, and, of course, I am “Z”. Everyone else is real, to the best of my knowledge.

Anne asked me some general questions starting with: “I would like to call your attention back to June 3rd, 1980 and ask if on that date you were moving into a new apartment? What was the address? Where had you come from on that date when you first came into the apartment?”

She was able to establish the fact that I was moving and had eaten lunch with my daughter at the Sir Walter Raleigh Inn before I went into the apartment. Then, with very specific questioning regarding the distance from the restaurant to my apartment, the time of day it was, if I locked the apartment door when I got home, we got to the part about the attack.

Harrington: Was there a particular reason your daughter wasn’t in school that day?

Z: She was ill.

Harrington: Do you recall who you called on the telephone?

Z: I called my answering service and I called my daughter’s doctor to make an appointment.

Harrington: What time did you make an appointment for, if

you recall?

Z: For 4:00 o'clock.

Harrington: What time was it when you called to make the appointment?

Z: I think it was about 3:30.

Harrington: What happened next?

Z: After I made my calls, I sat down on the couch, it was about somewhere, I guess, quarter to 4:00, then I went back into my daughter's room and I said, "let's get ready to go to the doctor". She had to get her shoes on and I helped her because she had a fever of 103 and was quite ill. We both walked into the living room and dining area, which was an L-shaped area, and she stood in the living room and I stood in the dining room and I suddenly realized that I had a pair of hands over my mouth that weren't mine and weren't my daughter's.

Harrington: What did you do then?

Z: I grabbed the hands away so that I could scream. As I did that, I screamed. I also realized at that time that there was someone in the hall vacuum cleaning and that my screaming probably wasn't going to be heard.

Harrington: What happened after you started screaming?

Z: We struggled and the assailant said "Shut up or I'm going to kill you." During the struggling, we both lost our balance slightly and fell down and both immediately got up and at that point he said,

"Shut up, stop screaming or I'll kill you," he started to go like that (demonstrating) with the knife...

Harrington: At what area?

Z: Towards the throat. I pushed the hands up and it went across the mouth (the knife).

Harrington: Where was Y (daughter) at that time?

Z: In the living room watching.

Harrington: How old was Y at the time?

Z: Eight.

Harrington: What happened next?

Z: I realized that I was dealing with someone who wasn't sensible, obviously , and that I should be fully cooperative instead of trying to struggle with this man. I said to him–this is after I had been knifed and I was bleeding severely–I said to the man "whatever you are going to do, you can't do this in the presence of my daughter", because I didn't know what he was going to do. I didn't know why he was there or what he wanted or who he was.

Harrington: What happened next?

Z: He said, "Okay," and he pointed the knife at my daughter and said, "Go to your room and shut the door and don't come out", and he escorted her, in a sense, part of the way and she went into her room. She didn't say a word and went into her room and closed the door. Then he said, "Where's the money?" I had thought I left my purse in the kitchen and I started to go to the kitchen to get it and I realized it wasn't there and I went around into the living room. He was with me at all times, pointing the knife at me. I got my purse, which was in the living room, and I took out my money, which was $20.00, and gave it to him. Then he said, "Okay, now take your pants off", so I took—I was wearing slacks—I took them off and he said, "Take your underwear off" and I took them off, too, and then I sat down again so he couldn't see too much—you know...I then said to him, I realized he had been in the apartment for some time, and perhaps he had heard my phone call to the doctor, and I said "my daughter's doctor is due any minute so if you don't leave you're going to get caught", so he said, "Okay" and then he left.

Harrington: Can you describe your assailant's voice?

Z: Yes, it was distinctive to me because it was a very calm monotone type of voice. It wasn't what you'd call a tenor or a bass. It was sort of in-between. He was pretty sure of what he was doing and his voice control was calm and steady. There wasn't much fluctuation in the voice.

She went on to ask me when I first became aware of the fact that he had a knife and how many opportunities I had to look at the subject. This was important because Harrington wanted to establish the fact that I had a good look at the assailant and that my identification was credible.

She had me describe his clothing and the sunglasses he was wearing.

Harrington: Describe your assailant for us.

Z: I would say he was between five-eight and five-nine with an olive-yellowish type of complexion. He had a mustache, coarse type hair, longish in the front and longer in the back, sort of a feathered type of effect. He was wearing jeans and a T-shirt and I also observed that his clothes were neat. They weren't sloppy jeans or a sloppy T-shirt. His sunglasses were a tinted color, probably the rimless type. The color would be somewhere between a pink and an amber. He was between 20 and 30 years old and maybe 140 lbs.

Harrington then asked me what I did after he left my apartment. I replied, "I just sat on the couch for a minute, where I was when he left, just, you know, just to think of what happened. Then I got up and locked my door and went into the kitchen and called 911 and asked them to bring an ambulance, and told them that I had just been attacked and I described the man on the phone and then they came."

And so the trial went. I was asked intricate details about everything that occurred that day, including the gruesome details of the three hours that I had to be in surgery. The knifing had been across the mouth, extending halfway across my cheeks. I could barely talk. For some reason, the doctors wanted me to be awake during the surgery, so what they did was inject drugs into my cheeks which numbed my face. It was terrifying to see them stitching my face, first the right side, then the left side. The jury could tell that I was visibly upset describing the surgery.

Later, during the hearing, I had to describe how I went back to the apartment the next day with Warren (and Warren's gun, the Luger) to retrieve my belongings and have my furniture put in storage. I also testified how I had seen the assailant a few days before I had moved in...he was the creep that I had pointed out to Charlie and Margaret, the creep that I had described to Jim, the general manager of the Holiday Inn.

It was a long day. When we were done, Jim drove us back home; another 70 miles through rush hour traffic. We stopped at a local café for dinner. Jim quickly had several drinks. I was proud of him for remaining sober throughout the first day of the hearing. And there was more to come, there was the cross-examination by the defense attorney. I had no idea of what to expect.

The following day in court I went back on the witness stand. This time there was a long interrogation about how I identified the attacker from the photographs that were initially shown to me by Detectives Neville and Williams, and how my daughter (Y) chose photos. The defense attorney made a big issue over the identification process and again, he argued about the line-up process. The attorney, Mr. Davis, said to the Court:

"As I explained at the bench, the fact that Z had had a previous opportunity on more than one occasion to make a photographic viewing is a fact that is coming to our attention for the first time today, and as I understand from the State, the substance of that testimony is coming to her attention at the same time. It was not the testimony of either officer—that is Officer Neville or Officer Williams, at the time of the motion to suppress previous photographic identification."

This subject, the viewing of the photos, was blown way out of proportion by Mr. Davis. I truly didn't understand his motive other than to confuse the jury and pull them away from the true issues. The fact of the matter was that I had viewed photos—7 or 8 of them—of suspects, on two occasions: once without my daughter present, once with my daughter present. On the second occasion, the photos were primarily shown for my daughter to make an identification, while I watched.

We wasted over two hours while Davis argued about this. It was absolutely asinine. *Of course*, he was trying to get the photos thrown out as evidence. The fact was—I identified X in the photos and so did my daughter. And I identified X at the line-up, and so did my daughter, and the judge let it stand.

Later, during the recess, Anne Harrington told me that she expected the trial to last about a week. I had no idea how I could endure a week of this stuff, but then I comforted myself with the premise, the idea, that X would finally get prosecuted, that he would get locked-up for a long time, and I would finally be free.

Then came the Direct Examination by the Defense Attorney, Davis. I didn't like him. Part of the reason that I didn't like him was because he was defending X. The other reason I didn't like him was because of his whiney, sniveling attitude, and because of that attitude, he had great difficulty expressing himself. His questions were confusing and he often had to pose them two or three times because no one could understand what he was talking about.

Davis was maybe in his late 30's and sort of plain looking; your average Joe type of guy, so it was hard for me to figure out where all of this arrogance came from. I tried not to let my hostility show, even when he got nasty.

He spent a long time, a very long time, asking more questions about the photo I.D. process. It seems to me that he was trying to suggest, that in some way, I made overtures during my daughter's identification.

"The only thing I am concerned about is whether or not you followed the instructions of the police and isn't it a fair statement that you didn't? I don't question your good faith in what you did. You made comments and you had a conversation with your daughter during the period of time when she was attempting to make an identification from those photographs..."

After he was done agonizing over this subject—the photographs—the Judge finally pointed out that it was nearing 5 o'clock and that Court would be adjourned for the day. I was beyond being relieved. I was exhausted from the process.

Again, Jim was our chauffeur and we had to confront the 5 o'clock traffic as we drove the 70 miles back home. We stopped at the same café for dinner because I was paying for it. I was very low on cash because I hadn't worked much as a result of the trial and I happened to have had a credit card for that particular café.

"How did you feel about the cross-examination today?" Jim was asking as we waited for the cocktails he had ordered.

"Yeah, well, that attorney—Davis—he's distracting the jury from the real events by arguing about this and that, about the photographs, about the description of the guy, about everything. He's trying to be intimidating—but I won't let him. Weren't you surprised that Anne didn't raise any objections to his line of questioning?" "No." Jim shook his head. "I think she wants him to make an ass out of himself."

Just then a mutual friend stopped by our table. She was more of an acquaintance like Jan was, the one who pursued Bob after we broke up. Coleen was about 10 years older than me. She was trolling for a seventh husband. We referred to her as our local "Elizabeth Taylor". Coleen didn't work—she earned alimony. Her last husband had somehow worked out a deal where her alimony was about to run-out in less than a year. She was desperate. “Are you and Jim an item now?” She had the nerve to ask. The café was one of her favorite hang-outs and she had observed Jim, me and Y having dinner there two nights in a row. “No, actually, we’re negotiating a break-up are you interested?” I replied. “Whoa...!” Jim gasped and laughed in one breath... “I’m not part of this meat market!” Coleen stomped off in a huff realizing that we were ridiculing her. She wasn’t terribly well-liked, basically because she was so aggressive. I had been friendly with her for a couple of years and sort of felt sorry for her. She was attractive for her age—tall—like me with short cropped platinum hair. She spoke in a slow husky voice which she had cultivated to emulate Greta Garbo. Her vanity plates on her white Cadillac said it all: RU4ME.

We had lunch together once—a “girlie” kind of thing and she had confessed to me that she deplored sex. During all of her marriages, she had been faking it big time, just so she could live lavishly—minks, diamonds and Cadillacs were the love of her life.

Jim and I laughed after she went away; Jim had told her a long time ago that he was not interested but because I was with him she thought he was game.

“She’s a trip” was all Jim could say. By now, he was on his second cocktail and I was having a glass of wine.

That night, Jim stayed at my place. Even though he lived just across the way, I was scared. The assailant wasn’t convicted yet and I was still testifying and was just plain scared. He brought a bottle of vodka over. I didn’t care, just as long as we made it to Court on time the next day.

We sat on the couch in the living room after I put Y to bed. Jim was guzzling his cocktail and I was watching the 10 o’clock news. He put his arm around me and suddenly we were passionately making-out:

kissing and all the rest.

We had been brief lovers almost two years prior and I guess the dramatic events of the last two days were culminating into a romantic interlude. I was o.k. with that until it came to my attention that he wasn't going to be able to perform. The vodka had rendered him impotent and as much as he tried while we were sprawled out on my brown velvet couch, he just couldn't get the thing to work. And he didn't seem to care, either...he just conked-out and went to sleep. I left him there and put the booze away so he wouldn't be tempted to take a nip in the morning.

As the hearing progressed to day three, I was beginning to wear out, but I was still determined to get the guy convicted. This time Davis had me back on the stand, and he was asking about when I had first sensed that someone was watching me while I was moving boxes into the new apartment.

"...as I stated previously, in the four days that I had been going back and forth, moving things on my own, I very distinctly had that feeling over the period of four days."

Davis: That somebody was following you?

Z: That someone was watching me. I have never had that feeling before in my life.

Davis: Why didn't you report it to the police?

Z: How can you report something like that? C'mon...that someone's watching me?

Just another one of Davis's stupid questions. A real waste of time. Then he asked me if I had told anyone else about it and I mentioned Charlie and Margaret and how we saw the creep loitering outside the new apartment a few days before I moved in. Then Davis got to the part when I was in the new apartment on the day I got knifed, right after we came back from the restaurant and I called my daughter's doctor:

Davis: Did you in fact make an appointment for 4:00 o'clock?

Z: In fact, I think I called the doctor in the morning as well, as early as 9:00 o'clock, and I probably called back for some particular reason, I don't recall what it was, but the appointment was for 4:00 o'clock, yes.

Davis: Well, before you were intruded upon on the afternoon of June 3rd, were you late for that appointment?

Z: We were leaving for the appointment at quarter to 4:00. After I had been knifed and hospitalized, yes, I would say we were late...we never showed up. (Duh!!)

When Davis got around to the description of the intruder, he mentioned that in the initial police report, I had described the man as being Hawaiian or Oriental, not from his eyes because he was wearing sunglasses—but from his brow—a broad forehead. So his line of questioning zeroed into the description of his brow :

Davis: Let me ask you something, ma'am. Would it cause you any distress to look at his eyebrows to determine whether or not you recognize any scarring or marks about his eyebrows today that you may have seen or may not have seen on the afternoon of June 3rd.

Z: I don't care to.

Davis: Would it cause you any distress for us to ask you

	to stand back-to-back with X?
Z:	*Yes*, it would!
Davis:	And to compare your relative height?
Z:	I will *not* do that. I won't go near that man.
Davis:	Let me ask you this, with the Court's permission. Will you come to the blackboard and with my assistance and the assistance of the State, maybe we can at least show markings against the blackboard so that...
Z:	I have boots on with two-inch heels so I don't know how that would help you at all. I said I am five-nine and in my flat shoes and I'm not going to be taking off my boots in court.
Davis:	I respect that. Sometime during a recess, if there is one, would you do that for us?
Z:	I will.

Davis continued his examination with what seemed to be a penchant to befuddle the jury. He would complicate every issue: The number of photographs used for identification , to minute details concerning the line-up that I had to go to. When I went with my daughter, Anne Harrington, and the two detectives to the facility where the line-up was being held, someone had left the door open and from a distance I could see X in full view in the room. It really shook me up because I was sure that he had seen me, too.

Davis asked me how far I was from the door when this happened. I told the Court that it was quite a distance, but even so, I saw X right away. I saw him, standing there, and then they closed the door. Then Davis asked me, "Did you know if he saw you?"

I replied that I believed that he had, and that they had me do the line-up identification anyway. Davis was actually trying to get the line-up identification thrown-out as evidence because of my seeing X through the door, but it didn't happen. The Court allowed it.

To complicate things further, he made a big issue over the fact that I had collected "Victim's Compensation". He made it sound as if I didn't deserve the compensation and that somehow I did some bartering to get it.

Finally, he ended his direct examination with a few more stunning questions:

Davis:	You indicated yesterday that you have not been back to the Sir Walter Raleigh Inn since June 3rd of 1980.
Z:	That's correct.
Davis:	Is that due to the fact that you haven't been in the area since June 3rd, 1980 other than to come for a line-up and to assist the State's Attorney and to appear as a witness in Court?
Z:	No.
Davis:	Does it have something to do with the fact that at sometime between June 3rd, 1980 and today you were told that X was an employee of the Sir Walter Raleigh Inn?
Z:	Yes.
Davis:	That is all I have, Your Honor.

Without his realizing it, Davis brought up a very incriminating fact: X was working at the Sir Walter Raleigh Inn on June 3rd. He was there while Y and I were having lunch, and later on, Anne Harrington would show the Court how X left the Inn right after I did and never returned to work that day.

Anne Harrington then proceeded with the redirect examination. She was very specific and basically re-emphasized the fact that before, during and after the attack I had ample time to observe the defendant and to therefore identify him. She stressed the fact that my daughter selected X from photographs and the line-up *without* anyone's assistance and that I had filed a claim with the Criminal Injuries Board in Baltimore at the suggestion of Detective Williams. She did this because Davis made it sound like I was filing the claim because I was trying to rip-off the State. Naturally, when Anne was done, Davis wanted to add his two cents, so her redirect examination was followed by Davis's Re-cross-Examination.

Davis: In fact, you received an emergency award from the Criminal Injuries Compensation Board at least before September 22nd, 1980, is that correct?

Z: Yes.

Davis: Isn't it a fact that you received the bulk of your award from the Board after a hearing with Commissioner Schmeling in early 1981?

Z: Yes.

And then he seemed to have an argument with himself about my reviewing documents that were presented to the Board. After that he discussed how I locked my door after X left and another brief discussion of the photo ID process, and I was given an opportunity to review notes written by the Board. These seemed to be redundant, nonsensical questions and again Davis was making an ass out of himself and wasting the

Court's time. And then he was done. It was almost one o'clock, so the Judge ordered a lunch recess for an hour.

Jim, me and Y went to the restaurant around the corner. We had checked-out the Court cafeteria and it seemed too morbid and you weren't allowed to smoke there. Jim was as much of a smoker as I was.

When we returned at two o'clock, Y was called to testify. Anne had told me that she'd be next, so she was prepared. Even so, I reassured her and told her just to tell the truth and not to be scared. I was amazed at how self-assured she was for a ten year-old. Jim was also impressed with her very articulate answers.

The direct examination began with Anne asking her some basic questions like what grade she was in at school and what subjects she was taking. Then there was the part about did she understand the difference between lying and telling the truth. Y calmly said, "Well, telling the truth is the right thing and telling what is honest. You get in trouble for not telling the truth." Upon that, Anne said, "I would like to proffer that Y is a competent witness."

After asking Y some questions about school, Anne went right to June 3rd, 1980, starting with the lunch at the restaurant and up to when it was time to go to the doctor:

Harrington: What did you do when she said it was time to go to the Doctor?

Y: I said okay and turned off the TV. I got my shoes on because I had my shoes off, and I walked–there was a chair by the kitchen and there were some boxes around it and I sat down there and was tying my shoes and my mom was standing between the wall and a table and chair in the dining room. I was done and when I looked up—my mom—the man was right behind her and he had a knife, and he took the knife, and it was between her neck and chin... Soon they fell back and I saw that the knife had cut across my mom's mouth and---

Harrington: What made you look up at your Mom?

Y: Well, after I was done with my shoes I was going to look up and tell her that I was done.

Harrington: What did your Mom do after the man grabbed her?

Y: She just fell back.

Y very calmly went on to tell how the man told her to go to her room as he held the knife near her face. She testified that she went into her room and waited because "I didn't want to get hurt or anything." She explained that she waited in her room for what seemed to be about 15 minutes until I opened the door and told her it was okay to come out.

Harrington: What did you notice about your mom that was unusual?

Y: Well, she was–I can't think of the word but it's a thing across her mouth and blood was coming out.

Harrington: Do you recall whether or not she had her slacks on at that time?

Y: She didn't. She had on her underwear.

Harrington: I want you to describe the man that you saw grab your mother.

Y:	Okay. He was wearing light-faded jeans on. I didn't get to see his feet at all. I never looked down at his feet or at my mom's feet or my feet except for when I was tying my shoes. He was wearing a light blue top. His hair was darkish brownish about down to here.

Y was able to describe his sunglasses and referred to his skin color as"kind of tan, like he had just come back from Florida."

Anne asked her about reviewing the photographs of the suspects with the Detectives and how she picked out two—one of the defendant and another one without the assistance of anyone. She was brief and to the point. When she was done, Davis started with his cross-examination. Again, the issue of the photo I.D. process came up and he made a very clumsy attempt to confuse a very sharp ten-year-old. He was going in circles, trying to addle her, and every time he did that she asked him to clarify what he was talking about.

Davis:	Sometime today or this morning or last night or during yesterday, did you talk to your mom about what was happening inside this Courtroom?
Y:	No.
Davis:	You had no discussions with her?
Y:	I was told I wasn't allowed to talk with her so I didn't.
Davis:	Did you have lunch with her?
Y:	Pardon me?
Davis:	Did you have lunch with her today?
Y:	Yes.

Davis: Was she talking about what went on this morning and yesterday?

Y: Not to me.

After trying to get her to say that we discussed the trial over lunch (which he did not succeeded in doing), he went on to extract details on how the knifing occurred. His strategy was to try and convince the jury that she didn't really get a good look at the assailant, but he failed at that, too.

For a ten-year-old she was remarkably articulate and corrected Davis every time he tried to lead her into confusion.

He continued to question her for another 15 or 20 minutes and finally he was done. The Court then asked Anne Harrington if she had a re-direct examination and
she did.

She wisely re-enforced the fact that Y had no corroboration during the photo selection process and that she could clearly remember what the attacker looked like, and then her re-direct was completed but the day wasn't done.

Anne's next witness put an ugly bruise on the case. He told a *huge* lie and then tried to rectify it. She called James Ward to testify. Mr. Ward was a construction superintendent who had been working on a nearby townhouse development. The company was owned by a group of Japanese investors, who for some mysterious reason, didn't speak English. Because of the language barrier (Ward didn't speak Japanese), Ward took daily photographs of the project's progress. The photos were then used as a "development report" for the foreign investors.

James Ward was in his late forties or early fifties. He was your basic blue-collar type of construction guy...a little pot-bellied, somewhat gray around the temples...a family man; so when he was put on the stand, we hoped he could provide an eye-witness description of who he saw leaving my apartment building after the attack. Instead, he managed to muddy the evidence and then later he tried to admit to lying about it.

He gave good witness testimony regarding the identification of the assailant. He was able to pick him out of a group of photos (prior to the hearing) immediately. He even provided some of his own photos of the apartment when it was a crime scene. And then when Anne started to ask him about the line-up he had gone to, this is what happened:

Harrington: I want to call your attention to March 31st, 1982, the day that we conducted a physical lineup at the fire and police training building. Do you recall that?

Ward: I would rather forget it.

Harrington: Were you there?

Ward: Yes, ma'am.

Harrington: And did you have an opportunity to look at an array of individuals similarly dressed?

Ward: Yes, ma'am.

Harrington: I want to show you what is in evidence as State's Exhibit Number 12 and ask you if you can identify this as being the line-up of individuals that you saw that evening.

Ward: Yes, ma'am, that is it.

Harrington: Will you tell the ladies and gentlemen of the jury what you did when you went up to look through the window at these individuals?

Ward: <u>Yes, ma'am. I am ashamed of myself, Your Honor, I lied to the State's Attorney and to the two detectives</u>. I did not pick out the suspect. I only said to them that one of the suspects there looked something like, but I immediately identified the man... my wife was with me and I have children the same age as this young...

Davis: I object! This is beyond...

Harrington: Which number did you say to a detective and myself had similar features at the time?

Ward: I said number three had similar hair and looked somewhat like the gentlemen in question on the day.

Harrington: Did you recognize anyone else in that line-up?

Ward: Yes, ma'am, I did.

Harrington: What person did you recognize?

Ward: The gentlemen third from the end. I think his number is five.

Harrington: And from where did you recognize number five?

Ward: That's the same man I saw on June 3rd.

Harrington: How sure are you of that?

Ward: I am very sure.

Harrington: Now why is it you didn't say it that night?

Ward: I really did not want to get involved in this case because I have four children, all about the same age as the gentlemen here, and I know how I would feel, as his parents feel, and I did not want to be involved in the case, and I figured if I did not identify that man that night I would not have to come and testify.

Harrington: Mr. Ward, did anyone come up to you following the line-up and ask you in any way to either change your mind or to change your position?

Ward: No, ma'am, they did not.

Harrington: How did you make this information known to the detectives and myself?

Ward: I called and apologized and stated what I had done.

Harrington: Now I want to ask you if you see anyone in the courtroom today that you had occasion to see on June 3rd, 1980.

Ward: Well, the gentlemen doesn't have a mustache and his hair is much, much shorter, but X is the same gentlemen I saw that day.

Harrington: Your Honor, I have no further questions.

Then the cross-examination by Davis got tough. He was going to use Ward's lie to his advantage and rightly so:

Davis: You are absolutely sure that the person that you saw had a mustache on June 3rd?

Ward: Yes, sir.

Davis: No doubt in your mind?

Ward: No doubt in my mind.

Davis: You would go to your grave saying that?

Ward: I'm sitting here saying it under oath, sir.

Davis: Lying is not new to you, is it?

Ward: It sure is.

Davis: Well, you told the State's Attorney a lie.

Ward: But I rectified it.

And after discussing the description of the suspect at length, Davis hit him with the lineup situation:

Davis: Well, you realized the significance of a lineup procedure, didn't you?:

Ward: Yes, Sir.

Davis: And that it was to assist both the State's Attorney and the defense attorney and the defendant with respect to the identification issue.

Ward: Yes, sir.

Davis: And it is your testimony that you deceived the State's Attorney?

Ward: Yes, sir.

Davis: You deceived the officers and you deceived the defense lawyers and you deceived everybody that was in that lineup that evening.

Ward: Yes, sir, I did. Willingly and knowingly, I did that.

After awhile Davis got away from the "deception attack" and on to the fact that the company he worked for employed many orientals and the attacker was initially described as being somewhat oriental. Then he went on to discuss a car that Ward had seen on June 3rd. That was important because X often borrowed a friend's car that could have been described just like the car that Ward had seen.

Davis: Mr. Ward, let me ask you these questions and

you tell me if you made these statements.

Ward: Yes, sir.

Davis: At 7:00 o'clock in the evening on June 4th, 1980, in the presence of Detective Williams and somebody else whose initials I can't make out, you were re-interviewed at the job and you stated that the vehicle you observed on June 3rd was definitely a '78 or '79 Pontiac Sunbird, yellow in color; that you further stated that this same vehicle occupied by an Oriental, probably a half-breed, had been in and out of the complex several times in recent weeks; the subject sits in the vehicle in view of the pool and tennis courts; stays 10 or 15 minutes and then leaves; canary yellow color; if approached, the subject leaves...

Ward: That's right, sir. I did make that statement but –

Davis: Was the statement true at the time you made it?

Ward: It was true at the time I made it and it is true now.

Ward's testimony probably helped to screw-up the case because of his lying. Even though he tried to rectify what he had done, the jury had a difficult time determining what was true and what wasn't true according to Ward.

Later on, Harrington was able to clearly and honestly put a yellow Pontiac Sunbird or similar model at the scene of the crime. Another witness was able to even provide a partial license plate. The numbers weren't exactly the same as the Defendant's friend's car—but very, very close. For years, I would be wary of yellow cars—always memorizing their license plates. In fact, I am still *very* much aware of yellow sports cars similar to that model.

Ward's testimony ended around 5:15 p.m. and the court was dismissed until the following day.

During our lengthy drive home, Jim and I discussed Ward's testimony.

Jim felt that regardless of Ward's lying, the car was good evidence and would prove to be even more important with additional testimony from other people. He definitely thought that we were winning, that X had no way of getting off.

I was getting genuinely depressed by the proceedings. After we had dinner that night, I told Jim to just drop me and Y at home, and that I needed to be alone.

I needed to reflect and digest what was going on. I knew that my testimony was good and that my daughter was truly a brave, honest and articulate ten-year-old on the stand. But after hearing Ward, I dreaded what would follow. X was pleading "not guilty" so he must have some kind of alibi. But there were so many blatant, uncontrived facts: Positive I.D.'s at the line-up, the fact that he worked at the restaurant where we had lunch; that he punched-out on his time card shortly after my daughter and I were there and never came back that day; that his best friend had a yellow Firebird or Capri that X often borrowed and that car was seen at the scene of the crime and the evidence snaked on and on like a reptile oozing its way through the courtroom.

I was glad to be alone that night. Yes, I was nervous and wary, but after Y got to bed, I stayed up a long time and got out my old friends: my legal pad and my felt-tip pen—and I wrote:

> I cry not myself away,
> To tearful men of deedless soul,
> Lest I should be of sightless gray,

By nights' unyielding darkness.

With vacant eyes, I do possess,
A haunted face of wordless thought.
In guilty dens of emptiness,
I cry not myself away.

In midnights' tomb I mourn the dead,
Lost passions of my spirit,
Lest I should blush in selfish red
With knowledge of my sorrow.

Within somber days I speak,
To fearful men of decayed means,
Who do protest their lies so weak,
And hide by this my darkness.

In a sense it was prophetic, but initially, I was referring to the cruelty of the justice system, where victims, in fact, become the accused and defenders of their existence. But I had a naive faith in our system, after all—what else did we have? We had evolved substantially from the Greek theory of law, getting to the point where we were suing our care providers for millions of dollars. That, in itself, is a volcano waiting to erupt.

At one point, when Davis was pushing me regarding my legal representation in the hearing, he was inferring that I was planning a civil suit against the defendant. Well it was the furthest thing from my mind. I was still dealing with my fear, and my need to feel "safe". Locked doors and windows did not improve my ability to sleep at night. I was still only managing four fitful hours and all the while thinking that when the trial is over, when X is convicted and put away, I'd be able to rest; to recoup my lost sleep, and to finally get on with my life.

As I understood it, we only had a few more days of testimony left. And it would be important testimony. After that there would be closing arguments and then the jury would deliberate, and find him guilty. At least that's the way I assumed it would go.

When we got to court the next day, the first witness to be called to the stand was a women who lived in the adjacent apartment to where I had been attacked.

Her testimony was good, but provided questionable identification of the defendant.

Like everyone else, her description of him was the same: 5'8" or 5'9", about 130 or 140 pounds, wearing jeans and a tee-shirt, carrying a paper bag, having a dark complexion, maybe Oriental or Hawaiian, wearing sunglasses and having a mustache. She had initially selected two photographs out of the eight that had been shown to her—one being the defendant. During the lineup, she chose two men as possibilities, again, one was the attacker. But that wasn't absolute, positive I.D., and it only helped a little bit. As hard as Davis tried to confuse her, she stood firm on her convictions.

The next witness was the mother of one of X's best friends. She was important because it was her son's car that Anne Harrington was trying to implicate as the mysterious yellow car that had been seen at the crime scene. The mother was called to testify because her son was not available. He was in basic training at Lackland Air Force Base. He had joined the Air Force about six months prior to the hearing; approximately when Neville and Williams knew they had a suspect: X—her son's best friend. Anne Harrington was able to establish that X would often spend the evening (stay overnight) at the woman's house when her son was there and then she directed the line of questioning towards the car:

Harrington:	Did there come a time when you purchased a car for your son, William, to use?
Mrs. D.:	Yes.
Harrington:	When was that?
Mrs. D.:	January of 1980.
Harrington:	What type of car was that?
Mrs. D.:	A Capri.
Harrington:	Do you know the year?
Mrs. D.:	A '76.
Harrington:	Who was the primary user of that car?
Mrs. D.:	My son.
Harrington:	Was it ever used by any other member of your family?
Mrs. D.:	No.
Harrington:	Let me show you what I have marked as State's Exhibit 25 through 29. Take a look at these photographs, and tell me if you recognize the subject in these photographs?
Mrs. D.:	Yes, it is my car.
Harrington:	And do those photographs reflect the tag number?
Mrs. D.:	Yes.
Harrington:	What is the tag number?
Mrs. D.:	DTW-556.

Anne also got across the point that the car was yellow. After that she was also able to bring out the fact that X would borrow this car occasionally. Mrs. D. claimed that she told her son not to let other people drive the car because of insurance reasons, but that, yes, his best friend, X, did, in fact, use that car without her knowledge or consent.

The next witness that day was Detective Neville, followed by Detective Williams. Neville's testimony (because of Davis's cross-examination) was long and drawn out. It was full of objections and details, but basically Neville described how and when he arrived at the crime scene: he had gotten there after several squad cars had arrived. He ordered photos to be taken of the interior of the apartment and the pictures were entered as evidence. He then had the place dusted for fingerprints. He described this process for the jury and how certain prints were eliminated because they were considered to be "latent". This became a big issue for Davis—the procedure of determining "latent" prints and why they were disgarded.

Neville testified about how he interviewed dozens of potential witnesses who were at the crime scene and how he and Williams finally went to the hospital around 8:00 p.m. to interview me after I had my surgery.

He stated, "I observed a woman in great emotional distress. Her appearance was that of severe lacerations and a slice wound to her face. Detective Williams and I both took notice of her wounds and drew sketches."

Davis, of course, objected.

The detective mentioned that after he had interviewed witnesses, he started to look for the yellow car—maybe a Pontiac Sunbird with a tag maybe starting with DJE. (Sunbirds and Capris are very similar in appearance).

When it was Detective Williams' turn on the stand, the same

things were discussed, but somehow Davis managed to bring the question of the line-up back into the picture. He was desperately trying to get the lineup procedure thrown-out as evidence because the door to the lineup room had been partially ajar at some point and the witnesses could look directly into the room. The judge did not allow Davis's objection.

Then Davis went back into the issue of the photo I.D. process. He was, at this point, grabbing at thin air. He was being redundant, and boring as well.

Finally, the day was drawing to a close. We were into our fourth day of testimony and it became apparent that the trial would go into a second week.

As usual, Jim drove us back home and we stopped at the Café for dinner. It was noisy and crowded that night. The bar was packed with the regular Happy Hour Crowd, and Jim and I both knew many of the people there.

Barbara and James stopped by our table. They were a local dating couple who were in their mid-forties. I was somewhat friendly with Barbara; our daughters were the same age, although Barbara was about 10 years older than me. She had led an interesting, albeit-sad life. She was born in Germany during Hitler's regime. Her parents were killed during the war and she was taken-in by a poor, aging grandmother. She told me that it was awful and she ran away from home when she was 16. Rumor had it that she wound up in Paris and was a prostitute; but she saved her money and escaped to New York while she was in her twenties. In New York she got a job as a domestic and put herself through secretarial school. After becoming a secretary, she met her husband: an airline pilot for a major airline that flew regularly to Washington, D.C.

After maybe 12 years of marriage and living in suburban Maryland, she filed for divorce when her daughter was about eight and she allowed her husband to have custody so that she could party. Barbara was an attractive, slender gal with short brown hair that was tinged with silver on the sides. From what she told me about her attitude towards food, I was convinced that she had anorexia.

Her relationship with Jim was nuttier than hell, too. She had said that she left her husband because he was boring. I had met him and he seemed like a really nice guy. With James, who was very wealthy and liked to party, she had a tormented relationship, one that drew-out her anger and pent-up emotions. She'd do things like slash the convertible top on his antique turquoise 1967 Cadillac or throw his clothes out on the front lawn in the middle of a snow storm. So when Barbara and James stopped by our table, we were amused. And apparently so were they. "What are *you* two guys doing together?", James inquired "We're having dinner" Jim flatly replied. Jim had a distinct disliking for James, but tolerated him. He wasn't that crazy about Barbara, either. They gave us ridiculous "Knowing" looks and walked away. They had no knowledge of the trial I was involved with. They didn't know about the attempted murder, either. "He is such an ass hole" was all Jim cared to say.

That evening we went to our own homes again. The next day , Friday, would be a difficult commute to the courthouse. There always seemed to be twice as much traffic at the end of the week.

We arrived just in time. It was 9:00 a.m. and the Judge was calling the Court to order. My daughter wasn't with us that day. I had her go to school because she had already missed almost a whole week and I arranged for her to stay at my neighbor's house after school. There was really no need for her to attend the rest of the trial because she had already testified and wouldn't be recalled.

I wasn't looking forward to the day's proceedings. It would entail the testimony of X, and X's mother and father. They would testify as witnesses for the defendant.

First they called his mother. She had an attitude: She was annoyed. The hearing seemed to be a nuisance to her and her lack of patience was apparent.

She was asked first about an injury X had to his leg. The injury was of significance because witnesses said that the attacker seemed to have had a slight limp. Mr. Ward seemed pretty positive of a limp, but since he had lied under oath, would the jury believe him?

Mrs. X said that he injured his leg in November 1980 while hiking on a mountain with friends. Then came the eerie part, the part that seemed to be too much of a coincidence (and there seemed to be many coincidences):

Davis:	Do you recall what leg received the injury?
Mrs. X:	I think it was his right leg.
Davis:	Was he treated by a physician?
Mrs. X:	Yes.
Davis:	What physician was he treated by?
Mrs. X:	Doctors Ackerman and Witte.

I was stunned. I was absolutely stunned. I turned to Jim and whispered to him: "Oh, God! That's my daughter's pediatrician!" Jim looked at me wide-eyed. "No way!" he said into my ear. "That's where we had the appointment on the day I was moving. We were supposed to be there at 4:00 p.m. on the day I got knifed." Jim shook his head, "This is getting to be platonic—he worked where you had lunch and he went to your daughter's pediatrician...I bet you he was stalking you for a long time..."

"Quiet in the Court!" Clank! The judge's gavel made me look up. She was glaring at me and Jim.

"Please continue..."

Davis asked her about when her son started to grow a mustache. She admitted that he started growing it as a senior in high school, but swore that during the time that I was attacked, he was clean-shaven. How convenient, I thought. Especially since *all* the witnesses said that the man they saw had a mustache, and he had a mustache when he was arrested and he had a mustache at the line-up, but when he appeared in court, the mustache was magically gone again. This is an old ploy; to befuddle the witnesses by changing your appearance. He also managed to gain weight and cut his hair short.

Davis spent a good deal of time discussing X's appearance with his mother, but then he *did* establish the fact that X worked at the restaurant. The Sir Walter Raleigh Inn; that he *was* a meat cutter and his work clothes: a uniform and apron were usually splattered with blood.

After that he called Mr. X—the defendant's father—to testify. I was surprised to learn that the father was an engineer at the IBM Corporation. He seemed to be well-educated and not at all edgy like his wife. But he, too, testified that X had no mustache on June 3rd, and that he didn't grow one until later in the year—maybe in November. Then Davis entered State's Exhibit Number 49 which was X's high school yearbook which showed the defendant without a mustache; and that was the end of the father's testimony.

It was X's turn to testify. I thought to myself—yeah, right, this is going to be good...a pack of lies. In his case, what's the point in swearing to tell the whole truth and nothing bt the truth? After Davis asked him about his educational background (high school graduate), he got right to the mustache:

Davis: Did there come a time in the recent past that you shaved off your mustache?

X: Yes, sir.

Davis: Why did you shave it off?

X: Because you asked me to.

Davis: So does your appearance, is your appearance today the same as it was on or before June 3rd, 1980?

X: Yes, sir.

Davis: Can you tell the members of the jury when you started to grow a mustache?

X: I started to grow my mustache in October of 1980.

And then Davis tried to make it appear that his hair and weight and general appearance in court was the same way he looked almost two years ago.

He went on to discuss the defendant's employment at the Sir Walter Raleigh Inn; what his duties were as a meat cutter, where he worked in the restaurant, and for some odd reason X used the word "blood" often in describing his job. He talked about how he always had blood on his clothes and underneath his fingernails, and he said it in a cold, chilling, Jeffrey Dahmerish way.

When Davis asked X about his transportation to and from work (he had no car), he brought up the subject of his friend's yellow Capri. X admitted to borrowing it at least three times a month. Then he tried to alter the statement to mean he borrowed it and his friend came along and that it was usually at night.

I don't know if the jury (or Anne Harrington, for that matter) was catching these little faux pas: Like when Davis asked him if he remembered using his time card on May 29 th, May 31st and June 1st and his reply was, "No sir!" But when asked if he remembered using his time card on June 3rd—he said "Yes."

Then came another shocker, at least to me:

Davis: You are familiar with the community known as The Overlook, are you not?

(This is the apartment complex where I got knifed—where he tried to kill me).

X: Yes.

Davis: And you had a brother that lived there at some time?

X: Yes, sir.

Jim and I looked at each other in disbelief. No one had mentioned that his brother had lived there. These coincidences were adding-up, there were just *too many* of them.

Davis: When did he live there?

X: I know he lived there in 1978. I am not sure if he stayed any later or not.

Davis then became more direct, asking X if he was at my apartment on June 3rd, did he break in or enter the apartment, did he knife me and rob me and so on and of course X answered "no" to all of these queries.

When it was time for Anne Harrington to cross-examine X, she became stern and alert to his little lies:

Harrington: Isn't it a fact that your hair certainly has been more straighter recently than the way that you are wearing it today? Isn't that true?

X: Straighter?

Harrington: Yes. Let me refer to State's Exhibit Number 23, when you appeared in a physical lineup. Isn't your hair at least straighter in this picture then you are wearing it for court today?

X: I imagine in my mind that it doesn't seem any straighter.

(A strange answer).

Harrington: How about in your picture which is in the photo array? Let me show you State's Exhibit Number 8. Would you say your hair is different, at least in this picture, than you have it for court today?

X: (Snidely) It doesn't seem different to me.

She did the same thing with his weight: showing photographs where he is obviously heavier after he states that his weight is the same, and denying that he's any different than in the photos.

Then she got around to athletics, naming all of the sports he was involved with and stating, "So, you are a pretty athletic fellow, isn't that fair to say?"

X: Yes.

When she got to the part about his after school job, she got him in another lie:

Harrington: Well, you only worked until the late afternoon, isn't that correct?

X: Depending on what job I did. I was in rib cut training, and that was at night, and meat cut was during the day.

Harrington: Rib cut training wasn't until July of 1980 and you were out of school by then, isn't that right?

X: Well, I was rib cutting also in June. I am not sure exactly when it started.

He was beginning to falter, especially when she discussed the use of his friend's yellow car. He said he didn't use it alone but she got him to admit that his friend sent him out on "errands" like going to the store to get beer. When Anne got to the part about his time card, he, again, began trying to hedge from the facts:

Harrington: One of the other things you were required to do at work was to present your time card to your manager every day for his initials; isn't that right?

X: Yes, Ma'am.

Harrington: I am showing you State's Exhibit Number 51. Isn't it a fact that you certainly *did not* show your manager your time card for Tuesday, June 3 rd, 1980?

X: Well, I don't recall.

Harrington: Well, do you recall or can you tell from looking at it whether or not you ever punched out on Tuesday, June 3rd, 1980?

X: I can tell by looking at it that I *didn't* punch out on

Tuesday.

But then he went into an elaborate explanation, which made no sense, about how you could punch out on Thursday or Saturday to make-up time. The fact was that he came in for work that day, late in the morning, just before lunch. After he saw me and my daughter there, he left without punching out and went to the apartment ahead of me, because I had stopped at my old apartment before going to the new one.

When Anne was done, Davis had nothing more to say, no clarifications, and the testimony of the defendant was done, and court was adjourned.

Outside, I stood talking with Anne, Tom Faye (my attorney), and Jim. Everyone felt that even though we knew that X had lied, that his mother had lied *and* his father too—there were just too many coincidences to overlook. We agreed that the jury must have been smart enough to put two and two together.

It was the end of the week. Jim and I were both exhausted. We just wanted to go home. After we picked up my daughter, I suggested that he have dinner at my place, nothing special because I didn't have much food on hand—maybe just some spaghetti and meat sauce. Jim liked that idea.

While I was cooking he went over to his place to change his clothes and get a bottle of his liquid nourishment. When he came back , a short while later, it was apparent that he had a few drinks at his apartment. His big Irish grin bared a set of fine white teeth and I could see that Jim was on Cloud 7 working his way up to Number 9.

I didn't care, I was relieved that most of this ordeal was behind me. I was the primary witness for the prosecution and my part was over, and it was Friday. Jim wanted to party, he was an Irishman, so every pitfall and every win was a matter of drinking to "it" whatever "it" was at the moment.

He filled his glass with vodka and a few ice cubes and raised his drink. It was time for the Irish proverbs—"May I never be beneath you, may I never be above you...but always in your bedroom..." (Yeah, right, I thought).

"Jim, surely, you jest!:" I snarled. "Of course, I'm jesting...it's *jest* that I'm a wee-bit tipsy and jesting is what I do. Jeez... c'mon, zee-lighten-up-we're out of the courtroom now. It's over and there isn't a hill of beans you can do about it. Here, have a nip, it'll take your edge off...wear it some other time."

I sighed. He was right. Although I didn't care much for it, I took a sip of his vodka, then I decided to make dinner. I loved to cook, it was the one thing that transported me into serenity, and I was good at it. Preparing dinner was definitely therapy for me.

We enjoyed a relaxing quiet evening: Jim, me and my daughter. We never discussed the hearing again and Jim stumbled home around 10 o'clock.

I awoke to the sound of my phone ringing. I looked at my clock—it was almost 9:30 a.m. I hadn't slept that long since I was in college, and I needed it after almost two years of nightmares and only sleeping two or three hours each night.

It was my cousin, Janet, calling me from New York. I had told her about the trial a few weeks previously and she wanted to know if there was a verdict yet.

"No, Janet, not until next week. They still have their closing arguments to do..." "Don't you think you should move back to New York?" "I really can't do that, Janet. My work is here. I've been living down here for almost eight years and my friends are here." "Couldn't you go back to Macy's and work there?" she pondered. "No, I have a business here and Y goes to school here..." "And you got assaulted, you almost got killed there!" she replied.

I didn't need this. I knew she was concerned, and was being motherly but it was not good timing. I quickly ended the conversation and told her that I would call her next week when the trial was over.

Then Y came running into my room, "Mom, Mommy, Coy's at the door and says he's found Pierre!" Oh, God, I thought, now what? Pierre was our beautiful blue-eyed white cat. He wasn't a Persian or anything, just a sweet white alley cat that we'd had for a couple of years. I had noticed that he'd been gone for a couple of days. Every night when we got back from the trial, I'd call him home, but he didn't come. I wasn't that worried because it was the beginning of Spring and the weather had been beautiful, and he was a "Tom".

I put on a robe and went to he front door. Coy was a neighbor of ours. He was a few years older than me, divorced and raising two kids about the same age as Y. She was sort of friendly with the kids but they went to different schools and only saw each other outside on weekends.

Coy wanted to talk to me alone. He didn't want Y there. I told her to wait in her room and I'd be in there to get her soon.

"I found him in the woods behind my place. It looks like he was hit by a car or something and someone threw him into the woods..." "Oh, God, Coy! How awful! God, that's so awful."

"I'm sorry. I'll take care of it if you like. I'll bury him or something if you want me to." "Yeah, Coy, that would be nice. Thanks a lot. Listen, I'm not dressed or anything so I'll talk to you later..."

I closed the door and between the strain of the week-long trial and now this—I just started to cry. Y heard me and came out of her room. "Mom, what happened?" I composed myself and gave her a big hug.,

"It's O.K., it's alright. He found Pierre. He died, but it's O.K." "He died? How did he die?, Mom, how did he die?" "I don't know."

It was a sad, tense, stressful weekend. We just stayed home. I did some laundry and house cleaning and Y and me played some games and watched television. I didn't sleep well after that. I kept wondering if the death of my cat was some sort of revenge on the part of X...he could of sent a friend or something to kill my cat while we were in court, but I had no way of proving it. He knew where I lived because it was on record at the court.

When Jim picked me up on Monday, I told him about the cat. He didn't think there was any connection, so I quietly sat in the car while he drove, steeling myself for the day's closing arguments. Anne went first:

"Judge Raker, Mr. Davis, Mr. Foreman, Ladies and Gentlemen of the Jury, we are now at the fourth and final stage of the trial procedure that I described to you, and what must seem like a very long time ago when we started this case, and you heard opening arguments of counsel.

And this is the stage at which I told you that you would have the benefit of the court's instructions on the law, and on the way that the jury evaluates the evidence. And you would also have an opportunity to hear from both attorneys in the case, who at this point would argue the case for you, and make remarks about the evidence and the facts presented, and the law, and to present their case to you.

Now, we have been sitting and taking evidence for approximately six days, we are well into our second week at this time, and as you know, we had a separation of four days between the first set of testimony, and then the second set of testimony heard this week.

During that period of time, I called to the stand nine witnesses, and the Defense Attorney called to the stand – I believe it is 13 witnesses; and in between the two of us, we have introduced well over a hundred pieces of evidence. And you literally have dozens and dozens of exhibits that you must go through.

And because that is a vast amount of information, and a vast amount of detail for you all to absorb and remember, I am very glad for the fact that all of you took notes; and were very attentive during the course of the trial.

And I think that you are going to find those notes invaluable to you when you begin your deliberations, and you try and reconstruct for yourselves and for each other precisely what it was that a witness said, and precisely what it was that you heard.

I have decided to organize my closing remarks to you in three sections, and I am telling you this in advance for two reasons. First, you will be able to follow what I am saying; and then for your own benefit, so you will be able to tell when I am getting close to the end.

That will be when I have gotten to the third section, and you will know that the end is in sight. In that first part of my remarks, what I intend to do for you is to recap what I feel are important pieces of testimony from the witnesses that I called to the stand to testify in this case.

I intend to do this on a witness by witness basis. I intend to recap only what I consider the important points, because we have already spent a good six days listening to what these people had to say. And I hope by doing this that I will be able to refresh your recollection as to what the witness said and testimony that was given.

Please bear in mind that I am giving to you my best recollection of what I have written in my own personal notes, and what I recall the testimony to be. Judge Raker has instructed you that if at any time your recollection differs from either mine or Mr. Davis', it is your recollection that controls.

Certainly no attorney stands before a jury and consciously misstates evidence, but there are many things that go on during the course of a trial – and we are taking notes, and we are looking at papers, and we are referring to documents – and if by chance anything has been written down incorrectly, please accept it as our recollection being wrong and yours being correct.

I will recap for you what I think are the most important pieces of testimony that we heard from the State's witnesses to the best of my recollection, and I will trust that you will use your own notes and your own recollections to compare that with, and determine the truth of what was said from the witnesses who took the stand.

You are also reminded that the questions that I ask, and the questions that Mr. Davis asked, and even the things that Judge Raker said during the course of the trial, are not evidence. And if from time to time we had difficulty with a witness, and attempted to ask a very clever question to get the right answer out and were not successful, that is not evidence and cannot be considered by you as such.

Only what the people who took the stand actually said in response to the questions, and not the questions themselves, can be considered by you; and, of course, all of the documentary evidence which you have seen over the last week-and-a-half, and which you will have back with you in the jury room to look at, to peruse, and to consider during your deliberations.

The second portion of my closing remarks to you will cover the law. In every criminal case the State is required to prove not only who did the crime, but first that a crime was committed. And I think that I am on safe ground saying to you that there are aspects of a criminal case that are not always contested.

Nevertheless, the State must satisfy you that all of the elements of each of those offenses are present in the testimony, and that a crime in fact occurred, and that you are convinced of the fact that the crime occurred.

We are dealing with four specific crimes, four counts. The first is assault with intent to murder; and the second is assault with intent to maim; and the third is robbery with a dangerous or deadly weapon; and the fourth is statutory daytime housebreaking.

Now, Judge Raker used the term elements in her instructions, and that is basically a term of art. We say a crime is made up of elements, and what we are really saying is that there are ingredients to each crime. There are parts to each crime, and in order to find that an assault to murder occurred, you must find that Part A was present, and Part B was present, and Part C was present.

When I get to that aspect of my talk with you this afternoon, I will go over the elements of each of those offenses, and direct you with particularity to the testimony that you are to consider that will satisfy you that the elements are present, and the crimes did in fact occur.

Once again I feel on safe ground that there will not be a big contest as to whether or not Z was attached in her apartment on June 3rd. I think it is clear that she was. She was in fact assaulted by someone who cut her, and that she was robbed, and that person broke into her home without any permission, and without any right to be there, and took money from her on June 3rd.

The third and final area of my closing remarks to you are going to deal with what is the real issue in this case, and that is was X the person who attacked Z on June 3rd, 1980?

I will point out to you from the evidence that it is very clear that he was that person. I will direct you to the portions of the testimony where you will find that proof in order that you can satisfy yourself beyond any reasonable doubt that he was the person that did it.

And I will also direct you to the factors and the testimony which indicate that his alibi evidence is not worthy of being believed, and does not deserve to be assessed with credibility by any of you in your deliberations.

Okay. To Part 1. Recapping the testimony. The first witness that the State called to the stand was Z. You will remember Z as a tall blonde woman, a fairly young woman. She was the victim of the offense.

She came and withstood a very long direct and cross-examination, and she was on the stand for quite a number of hours. During her testimony, she told you that on June 3rd, 1980, that was a moving day for her, and she was moving from her old apartment on Forest Road into her new apartment on Christopher Avenue in the Overlook development.

She had her daughter, Y, with her, and Y was sick that day. They spent the morning making various stops and errands, and the movers came to the apartment in the early afternoon. Following the movers delivering the furniture, she and Y left to go have lunch at the Sir Walter Raleigh Inn.

She said it was not an early lunch; it was a later lunch, but it was not a terribly late lunch. They had a leisurely lunch, and Y had a hamburger, and Z did not recall what she had.

After lunch, they ran a few more errands, and went to her old apartment on Forest Road, and then went back to the Christopher Avenue address, where she installed Y in the smaller bedroom so that Y could watch her black and white television while she wasn't feeling well.

And then Z continued to go out to her car to bring in the last few remaining items that she had left out there. She recalls that the door to her apartment was closed, but she does not recall whether or not she locked it.

She stated that as she brought the things in, she would set them down, and return to the car, and she made several trips in that fashion. Following her last trip to the car, she came in, took a few moments to relax, and placed a phone call to Y's doctor to confirm a four o'clock appointment.

She testified that at approximately 3:45 p.m. she went to Y's bedroom to tell her that it was time for them to go, and let's get ready. It is time to leave. And she told her daughter to put some shoes on, and that Y got up and took her shoes, and went into the living room area of the apartment.

Z was standing more in the dining room area, and Y was in front of her, closer to the door. It was at this point that a subject came from the rear of the apartment, and grabbed Z around the mouth.

Her immediate response was to grab the hands away and to begin screaming. At this point, she sees this person has a knife, and the knife is at her throat. He says shut up or I will kill you. She continues to scream, and the knife comes to her throat, and she pulls the hand with the knife up away from her throat, and she is cut across the mouth, opening up both sides of her mouth into the cheek cavities.

During the struggle, she falls to the floor. She realizes at this point that she has been hurt. She stops struggling, and gets back up, and she says to this man that whatever it is that you are going to do, don't do it in front of my daughter.

At this point, the subject, holding on to Z, escorts Y to her room, and says to stay in there and shuts the door. Then he asks Z for money. Z leads the subject through the kitchen and to the living room area where her purse is, and opens her wallet, and takes all the currency that she has – I believe she said she had a $20.00 bill and there may have been some others – and gives it all to the man.

And then the subject does a very peculiar thing. He asks her to remove her pants, and her underpants, which she does. He stands and he watches her for a few moments, says okay, and then walks out of the apartment, opening the door and shutting it behind him.

Z takes a moment to compose herself, puts her panties on, realizes that the door is unlocked, runs and locks the door, gets to the kitchen and gets Y out of her room, and immediately calls the police.

Z told us during the course of her testimony that she feels that she had about 10 minutes to observe this person who was in her apartment. She was in very close proximity to the man. There were no obstacles in her line of vision, no problems with her eyesight, no problems with her health.

She told us that she made many attempts to look at the person, although in an effort to save her own life, she told the subject that I am not getting a good look at you, and I won't be able to identify you.

She told us that she did that because she felt that her life was in danger, and that she did have opportunities to see the person who had assaulted her, and who had cut her.

Now, that day and over the next few days, Z was interviewed by the local police force, particularly Detectives George Neville and Ernie Williams, who were conducting the investigation of the case.

She told us that as she recovered from the surgery and the effects of the shock that she experienced, she remembered more and more details, and was able to describe her assailant more completely to the police officers as she relaxed a little bit following the incident.

They took notes during the times that she talked with them, and she remembers telling them a description of the individual in far more detail than their notes actually reflected.

Z gave the same description to all of us here in the courtroom when she testified. Approximately one year and four months after the incident, Z was given an opportunity to look at a photo array. Contained within the photo array is a photograph of the defendant, X.

Z selects X's photograph, and says to the police that there is something about this one. The hair is not quite right. He seems heavier, but this photograph looks familiar, and that was X's picture.

On March 31st, 1982, Z was given the opportunity to view seven similarly dressed young men who looked very much alike in a lineup situation. And she testified to you the circumstances under which she was able to view that lineup.

You know from her testimony that after observing the seven men for a very short period of time, she said that I don't need to see any more. I don't want them to do anything. Number 5 is the man. Number 5 is X.

The next witness that we called was the daughter of the victim, Y. You will recall that she is about 11 years old now, and was approximately nine years old at the time of the incident.

She described for you a number of things in addition to what her mother told us. She said that while she was sitting in her bedroom, she was aware of something whizzing by in the hall. She called out her mother's name, and when she didn't get any answer, she didn't pay any attention to it.

She described the assailant of her mother, and she told you that his shoulders were shorter than her mother's, who is approximately 5 feet 9 inches tall. She gave a description to you all, including a time that she said that she had to look around the room when the police were asking her, describing the assailant as having an olive complexion.

And she testified that it was necessary for her to sort of look at colors at the time in order to describe to the police what she meant when she was describing this man's particular complexion.

Approximately a year and four months later, Y looks at the photo array. She selects two photographs. One of the photographs is X. She tells the police that they both look similar, and both could have been the subject. She is not sure. She cannot pick between the two. When Y views the physical lineup, she is unable to make any identification.

The next person that was called to testify on behalf of the State was Mr. James Ward, and you will recall him as the older gentlemen who is the construction supervisor for the Aoika Construction Company, and he is in charge of building the Woodland Hills Townhouse Development.

On June 3rd, he was out taking photographs for testing out a new lens that he had gotten for his camera, because he was used to making reports by photographs since he could not speak or write any Japanese.

As he was doing this, he caught an individual in the view-finder of this camera, and his attention was attracted to this person, so that he no longer looked through the camera, but he watched the individual.

And what he saw was not particularly remarkable. He stated that the individual ran down an area, and then turned, and then ran towards an area where a car was parked. He lost sight of the individual, and then he noticed a yellow car come out of the area where he had lost sight of the individual.

He felt that he could have captured quite inadvertently this person on his film, since he had just been taking random shots all day. But when the film was developed, the person that he saw wasn't there.

He described to you all the subject that he felt that he had seen that day, and said that he felt that he would have had a good opportunity to see the man, and was able to provide us with a lot of detail as to what he saw.

Now, when this information was related to the police, you heard that they immediately took a photograph of the subject known as Dorian, and that is Defendant's Exhibit Number 18, if you want to refresh your recollection when you are deliberating.

And the police—this subject had come to their attention before, and so they took that photograph to Mr. Ward, and said is this the person that you saw, and he said, no, that is not the person that I saw.

The investigation continues, and in September of 1981, Mr. Ward is shown a photograph of an array containing X's picture. Within a matter of some three seconds, he selects X's photograph, and says that is the man. He looks exact. The hair is short. On a scale of 1 to 10, I give an 8-1/2. If the hair were right, I would score it a 10 out of 10.

Mr. Ward is also asked to come to the physical lineup and view the people who appear in the lineup. And you heard from his testimony what he did at that time. He went to the lineup reluctantly.

He did not want to identify anyone for a number of reasons. He did not want to come to court, and he didn't want to get involved, and he had a son the age of the person that he has seen. So, he told you that he looked at the lineup, and didn't identify anyone, but said that number 3 looks similar.

And then with great humility, he also testified to you that it bothered him what he had done, and he discussed it with his wife, because he had recognized the man immediately upon viewing the lineup.

He came into court, and he told you under oath that the person that he saw was the Defendant in this case, X. That number 5 was the person in the lineup that he had seen, and he identified him for you as being the person that he had seen on June 3rd.

Now, Robert Kornhouser is the young man with dark hair who

lived in the Woodland Hills Townhouse Development. This was a lovely day, and a lot of people apparently were out enjoying the weather, and he was sitting on his front steps when he saw the subject come out of a yellow car, and go out of his sight for a period of time, and then come into his sight for a period of time.

His attention was attracted to the individual because the individual parked in a friend's parking spot. So, the color of the car was right, it was a yellow car, but it was the wrong kind of car. Mr. Kornhouser believed it was a yellow Sunbird that he was looking at.

He got to view the subject for a total of approximately 45 seconds, but he never got any closer to the person that he saw than the front steps. He felt that he could not identify the man he saw by face.

Now, in one of those coincidences that happens, Mr. Kornhouser actually knows the defendant through the association of his wife with a dentist, through her profession. They had from time to time seen the Defendant, X, when he was at his place of employment at the Sir Walter Raleigh Inn.

And for that reason, he felt that when he viewed the photographic array, and knew this person, he could not make a determination. But he did tell you that even though he knew the defendant, the build of the man, and the appearance of the man was such that he could not say that X was not the person that he saw.

The State called Michele Purtrallo, a young woman with blonde hair, who on June 3rd was living in the Overlook Apartment Development. She was attracted to the person that she saw running from the area of Z's apartment because he resembled someone that she had already discussed with Detective Neville, in reference to something that happened to her, some crime that he had committed in which she was the victim. I believe it was a theft in her car.

So, she saw that person and made a mental note of him, because he seemed of a similar description. She also described for all of us the person that she saw, and the amount of time that she had to see him, and the distance that he was from her.

When she gave this information to Detective Neville approximately one hour later, he connected it with the fact that they had discussed the previous person, and then the very next day arranged for her to actually go and see that person. Once again, that person being Dorian.

When she saw Dorian from the safety of the police cruiser going into his apartment house, she told the detectives that that is not the person that she saw running from Z's apartment. She was given an opportunity to view the photo array, and she selected two photographs out of the seven, eliminating five of them immediately.

One of the photographs was X. She said that both of these people look similar, and she could not choose between the two, because the hair style was different from what she remembered. When Michele Purtrallo viewed the lineup, she was unable to select anyone at that time, but she told us in court that the coloring of number 5, being X, was similar to the person that she saw.

George Phucas was the young man who lived in the Overlook Development and who was out playing basketball at the time that this man went by. He gave a description to you of the person that he saw, and he even told you that he went so far as to run in the direction that the man had gone to try to get a tag number at the behest of his friend, Jeffrey Schwartz.

To the best of his recollection the tag number that he got was DTE, and I would suggest to you that he told the police officers DJE, and that was the tag that they attempted to check out. But from the distance that he was at, he could not be sure. He felt that he did not get a good enough look at this person to I.D. the person that he saw.

The State called Ms. Judith, and she is the mother of William, the best friend of the Defendant. And she testified that she bought her son, William, a 1976 yellow Mercury Capri, which he had during his senior year of high school, and that the car was purchased primarily for the use of her son, and not for any of the other members of the family.

The photographs of the car were put into evidence through her testimony that she said were a fair and accurate representation of the car, and the tag number that is apparent from those photographs, and which has not changed according to her testimony is DTW-556.

Now, the last two witnesses that the State called, and I am going to put them together in my remarks, because they worked as a unit on the investigation, are the detectives who were the overseers of this investigation, George Neville and Ernie Williams.

And you had an opportunity to hear from both of the detectives, and they described for you the various steps of an investigation. And through their testimony, you had a chance firsthand to hear what happens, what really happens, when an incident like this occurs.

And you know that they arrived after the uniformed officers arrived on the scene, and that there were approximately eight or nine police cruisers already present. The victim had been taken away by the paramedics in the ambulance, and their first order of business was perhaps two-fold.

The first thing they did was to secure the apartment, and to search for evidence, and to preserve the scene. The second aspect of their work was to try to find potential witnesses, interview them, and perhaps develop a suspect from their investigation.

In an attempt to preserve the scene, you know that they directed officers to come in and photograph everything as it was, and you have those exact photographs taken on June 3rd, 1980, in evidence for you to look at, and to peruse, and consider during your deliberations.

You also know that they directed other officers to attempt to lift latent fingerprints, and you had a little instruction in what a latent fingerprint is, and that it is actually the smudge that the oils from the glands in your fingers leave when they touch a smooth object.

And that by using a powder or a chemical, these smudges can be transferred onto a piece of tape, and then reproduced and identified, or compared, with a known print for possible identification.

They printed Z's apartment, and you know that the result of that effort was that all of the prints that they were able to lift successfully belonged either to the victim or to her daughter. So that aspect of their investigation led them nowhere towards developing a suspect.

You know that they then went out approximately an hour after securing the scene, and began to interview everybody that may have had information, or may have seen something that could be helpful to them in proving their case.

They talked to all of the people that you have heard from, and as a result of that, they tried to eliminate anybody who was not involved, but who they felt might have been a potential suspect. And specifically they were talking about Dorian.

They showed Mr. Ward, at that time, Dorian's photograph, and he said that was not the man. And then the next day, they took Michele Purtrallo to actually see him in person, and she said that is not the man. So, at the end of all of their investigation, based on what they heard from the witnesses as far as the description goes, they had no suspect.

So, what did they do in order to try and track down the car? Well, they were dealing with two descriptions of a car; one was a Pontiac Sunbird, and the other was a Plymouth Arrow.

They told you what they did to try and find that car. They asked people in the neighborhood to report Pontiac Sunbirds, yellow Sunbirds if they saw them. They got a computer printout of 30,000 Pontiacs registered in the State of Maryland. They went through that list, and made a separate list of every Sunbird registered in the area, hundreds of automobiles.

They organized a small battalion of uniformed officers to personally go out and find those cars, and let them know whether or not they were yellow or some other color. They ran the registrations on those cars. They compared the descriptions of the registered owners with the description they had from the people in this case.

They spent approximately two to three weeks on this, and at the end of this work on the Sunbird, they had no suspect. The investigation continued, and sometime in early September, Detective Williams obtained a photograph of the Defendant, X.

He placed it into a photographic lineup, and he told you how he did this; trying to select individuals who looked similar, the same age, the same hairstyle, the same facial hair, so that they would be similar looking to the picture of X that he purposely put in.

He then showed it to different witnesses. Mr. Ward identified X, and Z selected his photograph as being significant. Y selected two, one of which was X.

Michele Purtrallo selected two photographs, one of which was X. He then elected to place X in a physical lineup so that the people would have an opportunity to see not a photograph, not just one-half of somebody, but the whole person, the whole physical person.

And you know what the results of those efforts were, and you know that X was identified by Z , and also by Mr. Ward. In summary form, that was the evidence that the State elicited through the testimony of the witnesses, and is supported by the documents and the photographs which have been received into evidence.

Let's talk for a few moments about the particular crimes that we have charged in this case. All of the elements of these offenses come from the testimony of one person, and that is Z, since she is the victim of the case, and she is the person that was subjected to the attack, and also to having her property taken from her.

So, you look at her testimony to determine whether or not the elements of each offense are present and you are satisfied that they are present. The first count is assault with intent to murder, and at the risk of sounding simplistic, it is an assault, with an intent to murder.

And because laws are fond of defining themselves in their own terms, they do help you out by giving you a few other definitions. An assault is an intentional attempt by force to inflict injury; an intentional attempt by force to inflict injury.

An intent to murder is not the same thing as an intent to kill. An intent to murder is an attempt to inflict grievous bodily harm. Now, the logic of that being the definition is that if the person subsequently died, it would have been a murder.

So, we look to Z's testimony to try and find out if these elements are present and they are satisfied. Now, intent. Somebody's intent is normally locked within the brain of the actor. So, the law allows us to look to all of the surrounding circumstances to determine what their intent was.

And what is most helpful probably is to look at what the person actually did as a way of figuring out what they intended to do. Well, we know that the person said to shut up or I will kill you. We know that he put the knife to her throat, and we know that she ended up being cut totally across the mouth.

You know from Z's testimony that this was not accidental. This was not the result of some unfortunate mishap. She told you that it was an intentional act when she would not stop screaming, and she would not stop struggling with her assailant. So, I would submit to you that those elements are satisfied and that crime is present in this case.

Now, assault with intent to maim is made up of three parts, the first being an unlawful assault, cutting, or stabbing, and I would submit to you that we have a cutting in this case—and intentionally done without excuse or justification. Surely you know from the testimony that there was no justification or excuse offered in this case.

And with the intent to maim, disfigure, or disable? Well, it is apparent certainly from you having had an opportunity to see Z, and also from the photographs, that she was maimed and disfigured as a result of this incident.

And as Judge Raker instructed you, you are to consider each count separately, and depending upon your determination as to Count 1, that does not mean that you then don't look at Counts 2, 3, or 4.

Each one is a separate entity that you are to consider and to return a verdict as to each one as a separate entity.

The third count is robbery with a dangerous or deadly weapon, and I would like to give you an "also known as" because I think it is more common for everybody, and it is more commonly known as armed robbery. And I think with that name that you will be instantly familiar with it.

Once again, it is quite simple. It consists of a robbery, accompanied with the use of a weapon. And a robbery is the taking of property from somebody by force, or by threat of force, such that they are put in fear.

And accompanying that with the use of a weapon elevates a robbery to an armed robbery, or robbery with a dangerous or deadly weapon. Now, we know that Z gave her assailant the money because she was afraid for her life.

We know that she was willing to do anything at this time that he suggested to her because she was intent on saving herself and saving her daughter. So, she gave him this money because she was in fact, in fear. She knew that he was armed, and she had already been injured by this person with this weapon.

The final count of the indictment is statutory daytime housebreaking. There are three elements to this offense. It requires that there be a breaking into the dwelling of another, with the intent to steal goods belonging to another.

Now, breaking, once again, is a term of art, and it is frequently a confusing term for people who are not familiar with what it means when used in these terms. It doesn't mean that you actually destroy a part of somebody's house. You don't have to like throw a rock through a window and actually break it.

The breaking means an unlawful entry which you commit by having to move something in order to get in; and it includes merely opening a door held closed only by its own weight. A door does not have to be locked. If you have shut your front door, and an intruder opens it and goes in, that is a breaking.

It must be the dwelling of another, and here we have the dwelling of Z, with the intent by the perpetrator to steal property of another. Once again, we look to what actually happened to determine the person's intent. And what actually happened is that this person took money from Z.

So, I submit to you that all of the elements of the four offenses are present in the case. That the corpus delicti certainty of the crimes that we have charged have been proved through the testimony beyond any reasonable doubt.

Part 3, and the real issue in the case, is the criminal agent, X? I would submit to you that he is. And I would ask you to attempt in your mind to reconstruct what went on on June 3rd in a realistic fashion from the testimony that you have received.

But with an eye towards not what is happening in a sterile courtroom almost two years later, but what actually happened on the day in question.

I think it can be best termed as organized confusion in those first few moments after Z reached the telephone and was able to call for help. We know that police units were responding in vast numbers, and detectives were responding.

We know paramedics arrived, and an ambulance arrived, and we know that a lot of citizens were involved in seeing some aspect of what happened. No doubt the confusion and the excitement created the presence of many more people, and the two detectives arrived and attempted to put some sort of organization to what faced them upon their arrival at the scene.

In doing this, they began the search for physical evidence, but they also began a search for testimonial evidence by interviewing the people that were on the scene that had seen some portion of the event and could offer them some help.

And as you know, several people came forward, and you have had the opportunity to actually hear from these same people that George Neville and Ernie Williams were able to interview on June 3rd and June 4th, 1980.

Now, in evaluating the testimony as members of the jury, you are already equipped with all of the tools that you need to evaluate it, to weigh it, and to assess the appropriate weight, and determine the credibility that the testimony deserves.

And I think the tools that we all ask you to use when you perform this function are your common sense, your own personal experiences, and your own determinations as to whether or not someone has a motive to fabricate or to shade the truth; has an interest in the case; has personal prejudice or personal bias.

And if you use these tools to evaluate the evidence, I think it will be clear to you that the evidence of the State's witnesses, although remarkably consistent, was not so consistent so as to give the appearance of being either rehearsed, contrived, or fabricated.

What areas were there differences? Well, there were areas of differences in time of day, distance, height and weight, age, and–well, I think that is all the ones that I can think of right now.

The kind of areas where people aren't just real good when they are asked at some time later, well, how far was he, or what time was it, or how tall was he, or how much did he weigh.

But their testimony is remarkably consistent. There is no doubt that we are all talking about the same person that ran from Z's apartment.

We have got two kinds of evidence that connect X to this offense to prove that he was the person responsible for it. I am going to mention the first as being circumstantial evidence, and I don't want you to think of that as a dirty word, because it is not.

Circumstantial evidence is evidence that tends to prove a person was present and committed a crime, but it is not eyewitness testimony. It is something else; something else that connects them to the place, to the event, to the crime, other than eyewitness testimony.

So let's look at the factors of circumstantial evidence that link X to this offense. The first one is that he was working at the Sir Walter Raleigh Inn on June 3rd, 1980, and that is the very place that Z and her daughter went to have lunch.

We know that he clocked in at approximately 12:30, although we have no idea what time he left work on that date. He could have been at the restaurant at the very time that the victim and her daughter went in. We have no idea what time he left, but we do know that he had the type of job where his supervision was not very strict.

He was the only one working in that kind of capacity, and it was the type of job where he worked by job lots. He had so much work to do, and as long as it got done, they didn't care how long he took to do it, or basically what his hours were.

We know that he had access to a small yellow American made car, that being the car of his best friend, William. We know that he was able to use it, and that he used it without any particular pattern, and without any particular regularity.

We know that there is a similarity between the tag number on William's car and the tag number that was reported by George Phucas to the County Police Officers.

We know that the Sir Walter Raleigh Inn and the Overlook Apartments are very close; that there is a very short travel time between those two places, and very close to each other. We are not talking about any great distance.

We know that the Defendant was very familiar with the Overlook Apartments complex because his brother had lived there, and he had been to the place some 15 times, and certainly knew the layout of the area, and was familiar with the way the buildings were situated on the grounds.

Now, take that, those pieces of circumstantial evidence, and couple them together with the direct evidence we have, the eyewitness testimony that we have in this case.

When you look at the photo array, keep in mind that this photo array was put together not to be easy, and not to sort of point to the right one and have everyone else look totally different, but to be hard.

To make it hard for people so that it is fair to the person whose picture is in there, and they make it hard, and they make all the people look alike. And yet we have selections, one selection after another, either positive of X, or certainly some connection of him as looking very much like the person that was seen.

Look at the lineup, constructed with the same purpose in mind; to be hard. All the people look very much alike, and they are all about the same build, and they are all about the same age, same facial hair, dressed exactly the same.

And what is the result of that? Well, by Mr. Ward, there is a positive identification. Z. Who should know better than Z what the person looked like?

Now, you had an opportunity to see her so fearful that she comes into court with a hat and glasses to prevent herself from being seen by the man that she feels can identify her, and she knows she can identify.

Eyewitness testimony from the women who spent 10 minutes in a well lighted area with no obstacles with the man who assaulted her.

Ladies and Gentlemen, evidence in a criminal case is not a chain. You don't take each piece of evidence and make a chain, and therefore say that it is only as strong as its weakest link.

And so if any of the pieces aren't real strong, then it falls apart. Evidence in a criminal case is like a rope. Each piece, strong or weak, in between, forms a part of the rope. And the more pieces, the stronger the rope becomes, and the stronger it holds together.

I submit to you that when you review all of the evidence: the testimony, the documents, the photo array, the identifications—you will satisfy yourself beyond any reasonable doubt that the defendant in this case is appropriately charged, and I will ask you to return verdicts of guilty as to each and every count. Thank you very much for your attention."

And then, it was Davis's turn:

"May it please the Court, Ms. Harrington, Mr. Foreman, Ladies and Gentlemen of the Jury, not to be trite, but I don't have an outline. I will try to be as consistent in my closing argument as I have tried to be helpful during the course of the trial, and as I tried to be in my opening statement.

And reflecting back to the moment of the opening statement, I believe I indicated to you that two lessons would be learned in this case. One was something about the presumption of innocence, and you would learn something about the vagaries of eyewitness identification.

And I think through the last moments of the presentation of evidence that I have kept my promise with respect to learning something about the presumption of innocence; that it would be improper, and that it would be a violation of your oath, and that it would be imprudent, and that it would be just unfair to the system for anybody to formulate any opinions or conclusions, or feelings about the guilt or innocence of any person on trial with respect to any charge in the State until you have heard everything.

But the fact of the issue of the lesson of the vagaries of eyewitness identification, I think this case is the perfect example that points out all of the pitfalls, all of the pluses with respect to arguments, and all of the minuses with respect to arguments that any scholar, or any Judge, or any layperson could make with respect to the reliability of eyewitness identification.

Ms. Harrington has broken out her closing argument into three categories. One is a recap of the testimony of the witnesses. I am not going to take it witness by witness and tell you what my firm belief or my reasonable belief is for what each witness said is.

I watched you very carefully during the course of the trial. I noticed that you all were taking notes, and you were all attentive, and at times you were very helpful to me when I was trying to present evidence to you which I believed would be of help to you in your ultimate determination.

So, I am not going to recap what I believe each witness said, and when they said it, and I am not going to give you my opinion as to how I believe they said it. The law of the case is exactly as Judge Raker has given it to you.

We find absolutely no fault with any of her instructions; instructions with respect to assault with intent to murder; and instructions with respect to assault with intent to maim; instructions with respect to the robbery; or instructions with respect to the statutory daytime housebreaking.

Those are advisory in nature, and we would suggest to you that you not consider them in that light. But that you consider those instructions to be binding. I don't think there is any dispute that that is the law in this jurisdiction with respect to those offenses.

I would suggest that at the appropriate time of the State's final opportunity to argue the evidence to you that she specifically point up to you the positive factual evidence that she believes supports the conclusion that whoever was in Z's apartment on June 3rd violated the offense of assault with intent to murder.

As opposed to the positive factual evidence that she believes point up a conclusion that the person in the apartment of Z on June 3rd committed the crime of assault with intent to maim. I suggest that because it is the State that has brought these accusations against X.

And they have brought both, and it is up to them to satisfy you that in fact a crime occurred, whether it is a crime set forth in Count 1 or Count 2; and that each and every element of that offense has been satisfied by proof beyond a reasonable doubt.

Just commenting briefly on the evidence as I listened to it, and as I believe it to be, I think that the initial moments in Z's apartment were somewhat excited. I think there was an overwhelming sense of fear on the part of Z.

I think that in the struggle that ensued, when the intruder had his hands on her face, and she was trying to pull the hands away from the face, that somebody fell, or somebody stepped back, and as I view the evidence, and as I believe the evidence properly showed, it was at that time that Z was cut.

I may be wrong, but I don't believe that there is any evidence in the case that would suggest that after Z, according to her testimony, told the intruder, or after the intruder told Z that if you don't shut up that I will kill you, that she continued to scream and the intruder in fact cut her at that point in time. I don't believe that is the status of the evidence.

Similarly—and I don't know that it is relevant, but I don't think there is any evidence in the case that when the intruder left the home that he stood for a few minutes and stared at Z while she was undressed from the waist down.

I noted in Ms. Harrington's opening statement that was her representation to you as to what the evidence would show, and I have noticed that in her closing argument that she has stated that that is her belief of what the evidence has proven factually.

But I don't believe, and what my best recollection of what the evidence is, that there is any evidence to support factually that situation. That may have been, something that was told to her by Z in the past before the trial started, but we are confined to the evidence that has been presented in this case, and I don't believe there is any evidence at all to support that factual situation.

As for the robbery, there just isn't any dispute about the fact that Z was the victim of a robbery. And there is no dispute of fact about a crime of statutory daytime housebreaking occurred; that is, as those elements that Judge Raker has described to you are supported by some evidence in the case.

And I think the test is whether considering the facts in evidence, and the logical and the reasonable inferences adduceable therefrom, could you find a person guilty of statutory daytime housebreaking.

And as a lawyer, and an Officer of the Court, and trying to be helpful to you, I would suggest that there is evidence to demonstrate that a crime of statutory daytime housebreaking occurred on the afternoon of June 3rd, 1980. That is only half of the puzzle, or half of the burden that you have to assume in a few minutes.

The other half, which I think we all concede, and the half which is the most important, is whether or not X is the criminal actor, or the criminal agent, or in layman's terms, the person that was in the apartment on the afternoon of June 3rd, 1980, and attacked Z, and cut her, and took her money, and broke into her apartment, or broke out of her apartment, whichever way you believe the evidence is. That is the only issue in the case as far as we are concerned.

Now, it is a very difficult burden that you have, and Judge Raker, in her wisdom, and in her training, and with all the demonstrated confidence that I believe that we agree upon that she has shown throughout this case, has told you about the presumption of innocence, and the burden of proof.

She has given you a definition as to what the presumption of innocence is, and what the burden of proof is as it relates to criminal prosecutions, or the defense of criminal cases in your system.

I don't know what it is. I know that it is something that has to be right with each and every one of you. You have to be unanimous in your opinion as to the results of the case. It has to be something that you are willing to take with you each and every day from here after you leave.

I don't think there is any doubt that the last few days have been the most tense days in the life of X. I think it just means that you have to get together, and use all of your common sense, and use of your empirical knowledge; and your background and your experience, and your training, and your judgment of human beings, and your ability to determine what is fact and what is fiction, and what is real and what is unreal.

And if you come to a conclusion at the end of the case that X was in the apartment, so be it. But if you come to a conclusion using your common sense, and your ordinary training and experience that he wasn't, you have the absolute obligation to find him not guilty and to acquit him.

Now, we are going to be talking about some people. I told you in my opening statement that I wasn't looking forward to the examination of certain witnesses. I didn't have a feeling of delight or relish in having to cross-examine Z.

I had never seen her before. I saw a picture of her before the case started. But I was anxious about it, and somewhat apprehensive about it. And I told you that I might have to ask her some questions that might seem a little sensitive or indelicate at the time.

But I had to do it in an effort to be of assistance to you, and to be of assistance to X, so that you could have all of the evidence available to you at the end of the case to make certain decisions.

And I believe I tried to do it, and if I was inartful in it, or a little clumsy, hold it against me and not against X, who I am entrusted with the responsibility of representing, and who I have enjoyed the responsibility of representing.

Z, nobody can dispute, to the extent that she is a human being, was presumptively a very lovely being at all times before the mid-afternoon of June 3rd. We know very little about her other than the fact that she had a business of her own, and that she has a nice daughter by the name of Y.

That's all we know about her before June 3rd, 1980. What we know about her since June 3rd, 1980 is developed from the facts that gave rise to the situation in her apartment. We know that she was attacked. No human being deserves to be cut in the way that she was cut.

No human being deserves to have her apartment broken into and her money stolen, and to be bound up in the presence of her daughter the way that she was. And it would cost upon the best of human beings not to come away from that type of an experience without some serious emotional injury.

We don't know what it is. We know that from her testimony that sometime after June 3rd, she visited with a professional, whether it is a psychologist or a psychiatrist.

There was some discussions about masked feelings, and we don't know when that was. We don't have the benefit of the results of any conference, or consultation, or examination.

We don't know what the result of that experience was with respect to affecting in any way—either on the plus side or the minus side—her best recollection of the events of June 3rd, 1980. I think that the evidence shows, and Z shows, that she was trying to do her best when she testified in this case.

We know that she is very concerned that her identity not be disclosed to anyone, and she testified that she was very concerned that her identity not be disclosed to X. I don't think that there is any question that that was her testimony.

And she came into the courtroom with the glasses, and with the nice hat that she wore to preserve and to perpetuate that situation. I am a little confused by it, and I say this respectfully to you, and not to Z in a derogatory fashion.

Only because we have the advantage in the pretrial discovery phase of the case to see what she looked like, and we have obligations as lawyers to confer with our clients, and to go over the evidence with the client so that we can be of assistance to the client, and the clients can be of assistance to us, in the preparation of evidence, both in the defense of the State's evidence, or in the perpetuation of the Defense's evidence.

So, I am not exactly sure of the necessity, that is, the actual necessity, of her coming into court appearing the way that she did, but if the reason, and the sole reason, was to protect her identity from X, because her identity had long since been disclosed in the photographs, and the copies of the photographs that had been shown to us.

I am a little concerned, and I think the evidence supports the concern, about the fact that Z has so many lawyers. Now, I say that respectfully. I am not trying to say it in a derogatory tone. But what is the necessity of Z having so many lawyers?

There is a lawyer in the District of Columbia by the name of Sol Rosen. There is a lawyer in Annapolis, Elliott Newcomb, I believe his name is. There was a lawyer who was in court with her, and I believe he was with his son, and his name is Mr. Faye.

And there is another lawyer whose name came up by the name of Jack Quinn, or John Quinn, and Mr. Rowan, who practiced here in the city. I am just not sure of the reason for all the lawyers in her life, particularly as it relates to the incident that took place on June 3rd.

Does it tell us anything about her? I don't know. This is up to you to decide. They are not bodyguards, and it doesn't seem to support her stated reason of coming in with the sunglasses and the hat on.

Are they there to assist her in the perpetuation of legal claims against X somewhere down the line? I don't know. I think that is a reasonable and logical inference that could be drawn from the fact that she has seen so many lawyers.

The claims that she has filed. We have talked a little bit about the claim with the Criminal Injury Compensation Board. I endorse that claim process. It is probably the greatest thing the State has ever done for its citizens. That is, to make funds available for victims of crimes.

The State, like any other agency, just doesn't give money away freely without some demonstration that a crime occurred, and that it occurred in that State. And it requires the identification or some evidence of the identification of an individual that afflicted some injury, or some wound, or some damage to the citizen in this State.

And, Z, in filing the claim on her own, submitted the description that was reflected in the article in the *Gazette Newspaper*. The description was exactly the same as the description that she gave to the police on June 3rd.

She also submitted as part of her claim the description, that is, the written description that was a part of her report to the police on June 3rd. Now, does that mean that that is every fact and every detail that was in her mind in late 1980 concerning the identification of the person?

That is up for you to decide. The only thing that it does suggest, or at least that it does suggest, is the fact that she has adopted and endorsed that description as part of her own for filing a claim under oath with the Criminal Injury Compensation Board.

Is it just an indication that under ideal circumstances she is willing to put her stamp, her personal stamp of approval, on a statement of a given fact? Well, maybe it is. Is it supported by other evidence that was brought out in her direct or cross-examination testimony? Possibly.

We had some discussion with her about an issue of the claim, or a part of her claim, a line item on her claim. And that is lost wages or lost income for the period of time for the initial disability when she wasn't able to work. And it was a substantial claim, a claim of two, three, or four thousand dollars, or whatever it was.

I was very happy that she got it, and I am sure that she needed it. The thing that causes me some concern as I view the evidence is that in a succeeding suit that was filed in this Court on March 22nd of this year, 1982, based upon an event that took place on March 22nd, 1979, under her signature she makes a claim and states that since March 22nd 1979, as a result of the injuries to her daughter, she has sustained and will continue to sustain lost income.

Now, it was suggested to her on cross-examination that maybe this indicates an unconscious good faith effort to make this claim. I don't know if it does. But it is a fact that I brought to your attention to demonstrate that under a set of circumstances, or within a given set of facts, she might be inclined to endorse or might be inclined to adopt a position that was suggested to her by others, or a position that might be documented in the form of some piece of paper that she was looking at.

Now, how is that relevant to this case? It is relevant because her initial description to the police, regardless of what her physical condition was, is that of an oriental male, mustache over the corner of the mouth, half-oriental, yellowish skin, dark brown hair over the ears, amber colored sunglasses, nervous speech and manner, 28 to 30 years, 5 foot 8 inches, blue jeans, shirt, unknown.

If, and under any circumstances, had you not heard one fact in this case, and you saw X on the streets of the County, would you come to an opinion or a conclusion that he was oriental, or half-oriental, is going to require quite a mental exercise for you to answer that question.

I have been through that process myself, and I know that it is difficult. I told Mrs. X, that is, X's mother, early on in the case that we were in trouble.

Using another example, if someone told you before this case started that I was half-oriental, and you looked at me last Monday, and Tuesday, and Wednesday, and this Monday, and Tuesday, and Wednesday, if you looked at me hard enough, and you reflected upon what somebody told you earlier, it is easy to come to a conclusion that I might have an oriental background. And I would disclaim it.

And there is no evidence in this case on the part of the State that X has an oriental heritage, an oriental background, whether full, half, or part. Every single witness in this case in giving a description to the police identify the person that they saw as being oriental, or Polynesian, in appearance.

The mustache. We asked him to shave his mustache, and that is the evidence, before the trial started. So, that you would have an opportunity to make an independent decision, and hopefully unanimously, because his facial appearance today is the same as it was during the months of May, June, and July of 1980.

And there are just photographs, after photographs, after photographs, that show during the months of April, May, June, and July of 1980, that he didn't have any mustache. One so recently to the date of the incident, that is, May 30th, 1980, when he went to his prom. There just is no evidence of any facial hair or any mustache.

Now, height. Well, whether you are 5 foot 6, or whether you are 5 foot 10, under an excited set of circumstances it is not going to make a lot of difference. Whether you are sitting down or looking up, whether you are standing in the lower level looking up a hill, or whether you are even standing side by side, it is not going to make a great deal of difference.

Weight. Now, weight might make a difference. The description concerning the individual by those witnesses is in excess of X's weight, 135 to 140 pounds. His appearance is entirely different. The only possible similarity is the color of the hair.

Every witness that testified, testified that the hair was straight in some fashion, whether it is combed back, or straight on the sides, or whether it is parted in the center, the hair is straight. And it is not nape, not curly, and there is no evidence that he had a permanent before the trial or anything like that.

And you can look at the photographs to make a determination as to whether or not the hair that was described by the witnesses, and as you have written it down, is the same as the hair that was worn by X, and depicted in the photographs that you have seen.

The limp. There is evidence that the person that was in the area of the Overlook development on June 3rd had a limp. And the evidence from the State's point of view would try to suggest that X had a limp sometime during the month of June of 1980. There just is not any evidence of that.

All the evidence is that he had a limp as a result of a leg injury that he sustained in November of 1980 when he was on a hiking trip in the Sugar Loaf Mountain area of this State.

You know, had the State wanted to, they could have called Sonny, who was with X at the time, to testify that it took place in November of 1979, or May of 1979, or May of 1980, but they didn't. And they didn't because the irrefutable evidence is that he had a leg injury in November of 1980.

The car. I am very, very concerned about the car as I view that evidence. There is just no evidence in this case by any witness that the car was a Mercury Capri. And I think that the identification of a car is a rather significant piece of evidence in the case, because the person that is seen throughout that day is directly visually followed into the car, and the car drives off.

Mr. Kornhouser, who knows his cars, is positive that it was a Pontiac Sunbird. Our wonderful Mr. Ward, on the day of his interview on June 4th, 1980, says there is no doubt about it that it was a Pontiac Sunbird. The evidence from the police is that it was a Pontiac Sunbird, beginning with the initials that they spent so much time investigating for the many weeks succeeding June 3rd, 1980.

There is absolutely no evidence that puts X at any time in his lifetime with any Pontiac Sunbird, whether it be yellow, or white, or black, or blue. Or a Plymouth Arrow for that matter. If you look to the testimony of George Phucas, or if you look at the testimony of Jeffrey Schwartz, there just is no evidence that puts X with a yellow Plymouth Arrow.

But unfortunately X has a lifetime, longtime friend, by the name of William, who just happens to have a yellow car, and it is a Mercury Capri. You will look at those photographs and the State says the tag numbers are similar. We would argue that the tag letters or the tag numbers are not similar or familiar at all.

That is as much as night and day, and that the letters are a million light miles away, in terms of letters. They would not have spent so much time and so much effort looking for a registration with those three letters if they didn't have a good faith and reasonable belief that those were the letters on the tag at the time that the car drove off.

The only problem is that they did not look long enough or far enough. For some reason, they limited the area of their investigation to those cars that had registration information in the County. They spent an enormous amount of manpower, and an enormous amount of time, and not to mention at taxpayer's expense, in trying to look for the car.

But nobody, nobody made an effort to even dial 411 for Columbia, or for Towson, to see if there was a number for the person whose name appeared on the registration information that they had available in June, or July, or August, or September of 1980, whichever the time was.

And that since the date of June 3rd, 1980, and through the testimony or through the conclusion of Mr. Neville's testimony, he had not done anything more with respect to determining the identification of that vehicle.

The State is going to say, well, if that is such a big deal, Peter, why didn't you do it. Well, there is no evidence in the case as to what we did or what we didn't do. The only evidence in the case is that that information was given to us last Wednesday.

And if I have not accomplished in a few days what the State should have accomplished in almost two years, don't hold it against X. Hold it against me. I am a little embarrassed by it, but don't hold it against X.

I think the evidence unequivocally supports a yellow Pontiac Sunbird with that tag letter situation. And what about Mr. Ward and that car? It is a nice time to talk about Mr. Ward. We know that he is a liar. Nobody likes a liar, least of all counsel in a proceeding as important as this. But he is a liar.

I don't adopt, and I don't think that the evidence supports a conclusion that he came into this courtroom with a humble and a remorseful attitude about what took place on March 31st, 1982. I don't think it is supported.

If you look back on his testimony, Mr. Ward is a dangerous and untrustworthy witness. Forget about what happened on March 31st. Let's talk about how he responded, or failed to respond, to questions that were put to him. He just would not give an inch.

When he was confronted with his own statement that he gave to the police on June 3rd, and on June 4th, he wouldn't even admit that that was the written statement that he gave to the police. He would not even admit that the yellow car that he saw on June 3rd was the same yellow car that he told the police in his own written statement that the police wrote down that he saw on the previous day .

He would not even admit that on those previous days that the person never got out of the car, and that as somebody would approach the car, the person would drive off. And that the only time the person got out of the car for the first time was on June 3rd.

He wouldn't even admit his own statement. That is a sign of great resistance, and that is a sign of great importance in your ability, and in your obligation, to determine his credibility. He wouldn't even concede that Mr. Lee was oriental.

I was over here next to him, and I asked him to look over and to tell us whether or not Mr. Lee was oriental, and he said no. Now, using your common and ordinary sense, I think we would all agree that if he is not oriental, he certainly has those features that we would reasonably believe to be the features of a human being that has some oriental heritage or background.

But Mr. Ward would not concede that. But on June 3rd, what is he doing? Well, he is taking photographs. He is taking photographs of the job site because he doesn't speak the tongue of his superiors in the company.

He is shooting some photographs of women playing tennis, and all of a sudden through the gate, he sees a person, and he testified initially that the person saw him, and after seeing him, took off running.

He doesn't say that on cross-examination. But on his direct examination that was his testimony. On cross-examination, he can't say that the person saw him. The only thing he says is that the person came through the gate, and he ran down the side of the hill, and out of sight.

He testified that he got a good look, but he doesn't testify that, well, I'll withdraw that. But with respect to that testimony, and your obligation to determine what weight to give it, and the credibility of it, look at the testimony of Mr. Phucas, the State's witness, and Mr. Schwartz, also a witness for the State.

The testimony is that the intruder was a person of oriental features, and the description that you have is that he had a paper bag in this hand, and that he ran between the tennis court area and the swimming pool area.

And if Mr. Ward, and take your time and use your common sense, but if Mr. Ward is over in an area to the left, and which he described and pointed out, what he would have to do would be to look through two, 10 foot high, chain linked fences to see the person running in this direction.

And I don't think there is any evidence that there is a fence down in this area. There was some concern—and I made a point of trying to help you by asking Michele Purtrallo when she testified, about what she observed when the person ran up the hill.

And did the person run in the area to the right or to the left, and she was not able to say, because she never saw the person go over the hill. So, the more exact evidence on the point is from the witness' focus is that this person ran up the hill in an area closest to the tennis courts, well not the tennis courts, but the basketball courts, and behind the basketball net, and through the tennis court area; that is, the fenced area between the tennis court and the swimming pool.

And I think that objectively that is the realistic evidence in the case. I don't know what he saw, but I don't think the evidence supports that he saw X. Look at his initial statement to the police when he was shown the—well, not his initial statement to the police, but the testimony of what he said when he was shown the photographs that contained the photograph of X.

It is not a situation, and I hope that you took copious notes where he said that this is the man. I am not trying to mislead you. My recollection is that is what the testimony is, and I examined him specifically on it, was that he said that of all of the photographs, that was it.

His testimony ingests the position to Detective Williams' testimony is that he is asked something about a scale of 1 to 10. He rates it as an 8-1/2. And it is because of the appearance of the hair in Number 6 that I am not positive.

That statement, ladies and gentlemen, based upon the amount of time he had to observe whoever it was he was seeing on June 3rd, and the circumstances of that photographic situation, discloses that it was not a positive identification at all.

Isn't a little remarkable that after 14 months that somebody only needs three seconds to pick out a photograph. Does that tell you something about that person? Does it tell you something about the man? The victim herself and her daughter spent many, many minutes over these photographs, as did everybody else that looked at them.

Is Mr. Ward just the type of person that would say anything at any time, and under any circumstances, just to get it out? And then at the appropriate time, try to give somebody a bad time just to get out of the situation?

Now, he said something very interesting about March 31st. We know, and I think it is a very unpleasant fact to all of us, that he lied. That is, he testified that he lied about March 31st. It is not a situation where he lied to save X.

I mean, he could have gone and he could have said that I don't see anybody, and I don't recognize anybody. But you heard Detective Williams, and that's not what he said. He pointed out Number 3.

Now, what kind of person is it that would do such a horrible thing, and we know, or at least we have some minimal experience about the vagaries of eyewitness identification; where somebody would come in and say they lied about Number 5, and implicate Number 3.

Who is this Mr. Ward and what kind of person is he, and who is he trying to protect? You know, what does the evidence suggest in terms of facts and emphasis? Is it somebody in his company? Is he just trying to have a good time at everybody's expense? I don't know.

Why did he go back on March 31st? Why didn't he tell Detective Williams at that time when he asked for directions that he lied. I don't know. But that is the kind of witness that has testified in this case.

The distance. Your notes will reflect what his testimony is as to the distance between him and whoever the person was that was running in the area that he described. I think we can all agree that if the witnesses, if Phucas and Schwartz believed, that whatever distance it is, it is not as close at any point in time as the proximity between whoever the person was, the intruder, and Mr. Schwartz, and Mr. Phucas on the afternoon of June 3rd. I don't think there is any doubt about that.

I don't think that there is any benefit at all in the testimony of Ms.

Purtrallo. She is a nice lady. She tried to do her best, and I don't think there is any dispute about that. She doesn't make an identification of anybody, and doesn't make a positive identification of anybody, and didn't make any in-court identification of anybody.

I think she was just trying to be of help to indicate where she was, and what she was doing. And she was of help to us to establish that the person that ran from the rear area of 423 was the same person that ultimately ran up the hill to the area where Mr. Phucas and Mr. Schwartz were at the time they made their observations.

And she had a similar description. That the person was oriental, and the same height, dark hair, mustache, blue jeans, and the bag. And the bag is kind of important, just to make sure that we are all looking at the same person, and I was happy to hear in the State's closing address to you that we are talking about the same person.

Mr. Kornhouser. Mr. Kornhouser stated that he did not get a look at the face, and he can't say that it is X, and he can't say that it isn't X. But it is of some help to you in reviewing his testimony to learn that the point—that is, the geographic point of his observations of the individual when the individual returns to the car, is in the area of the end of the tennis court that is shown in Defendant's Exhibit Number 8.

Now, we have absolutely no activity for a period of 14 months. There were some photographs that are shown of Dorian to Michele Purtrallo, and photographs that are shown to Mr. Ward just shortly after the incident. But we have no activity. We have no photographic viewing.

Z says that she offered to do a sketch, and to participate in a composite sketch, and Detective Williams says that was not the case, and it was never done. But the fact of the matter is that there was little or nothing done with respect to this investigation between that point in time.

Should the Defendant be placed in a point of detriment because 14 months have passed and records that would more substantially account for his whereabout are no longer in existence, and no longer available for him to review, and no longer available for us to present? Take that into account, a 14 month period of time.

Use your common sense, and if you haven't done it already in this case, try and think about where you were at three o'clock or four o'clock on the afternoon of June 3rd, 1980. And if you had to, could you account for it?

And how many people could you realistically produce that would support where you were and what you were doing? It is very, very difficult, even with the availability of all of the documents. But when you have no documents, it makes it a much more difficult task.

But the State said that we have not demonstrated it, where we are. They said we were at 423 Christopher Avenue. Well, what is the positive evidence in the case as it relates to X? Well, the positive evidence is that he is an 18 year old boy. He is a graduating senior. He just attended his senior prom.

The State is going to say, and she has the right to say it, and she would argue that I am trying to appeal to your bias or to your passion, or to any prejudice, and develop some prejudice.

You have to judge the individual that is on trial, and not just the color of his hair, the kind of shoes or clothing that he wears, but his overall makup in making a determination if he is the type of person that would be engaged in that type of activity at that time.

And I would suggest to you that the evidence would support the conclusion that he is not. He is at school from 9:00 to 11:00 in the morning, and that is of significance, because the best witness in the case, as we believe the evidence showed, is Mr. Jeffrey Schwartz, who said that the person is in and about the area at 10:30 in the morning, and it is same person that he saw late in the afternoon, 3:30 or 4:00, or 4:30.

It was the same person, and we all know, and it is not a complicated process, to come to a conclusion that you can't be in two places at one time. We know that he punched in for work. Okay. That does have some significance. The State says that X would have had an opportunity to see Z and her daughter.

I agree with that. But let's look at it in the reverse. Z and her daughter may have had an opportunity, and in all probability had an opportunity, to see X. It may just be the last male they saw that day before the incident that took place between 4:00 and 4:30.

And in viewing the evidence, and making decisions about eyewitness identification, that is a very important thing for you to consider. On any prior occasion did the witness have an opportunity to see the individual that he or she described in determining whether or not the identification is a result of something that she saw at the moment that it happened, or as a result of something that she saw at a previous point in time.

X was never asked whether or not he saw them in the Sir Walter Raleigh Inn at 12:30 in the afternoon on June 3rd. We asked him whether he had ever seen them before, and he said no. It is up to you to determine whether or not he was telling the truth as to that fact, or whether he is deceiving you under oath, and lying under oath, and committing perjury under oath with respect to that question and the answer that he gave.

All right. Now, are we limited to just June the 3rd? Before the case started, we thought we were, but not having the benefit of seeing in person, or interviewing in person, Z, we found out during the course of her testimony that it wasn't.

And that's because she believes that she saw or she believed that she was being watched by the person on Sunday, June 1, and on Saturday, May 31st, and on Thursday, May 29th. Now, regardless of what conclusions you draw about the time record on June 1st, there is one problem in any way, shape, or form with any time record on Thursday, May 29th, on Saturday, May 31st, or on Sunday, June 1.

And those records are there for you to look at. You will have to use that little conversion table so that you can figure out what the period of time is, but Mr. Tonayko testified under oath that on each day—Thursday, Saturday, and Sunday, X was there for a substantial period of time; whether it is 3-1/2, or 4-1/2 or 5 hours. The bulk of the day.

Again, a person cannot be in two places at the same time. He can't be sitting in a yellow Sunbird out in the parking lot of Woodland Hills, and then working at the Sir Walter Raleigh Inn. It just cannot happen. And he took the stand and testified under oath, and it is up to you to decide the weight to give his testimony, just like any other witness.

You are the judges of his credibility, and you are the judges of the facts in the case as to whether he is telling the truth. It is going to be a very difficult task I would suggest to you with all of this evidence to make a determination whether a witness on trial in this kind of case is telling the truth.

But it would have to be a very difficult task to determine whether somebody of X's age, status, and mind, is telling the truth. Because if you don't know where you are, and no one can testify with any degree of certainty, or any degree of exactness, where you are at a given point in time, how are you going to be able to get that position over to a jury when there is nothing to support it other than the records that are no longer there?

And what happens, and what documents should a witness have

to be exposed to after 14 months, or 20 months, of the passage of time in that type of situation? And did he get up and start crying, and start screaming, that I didn't do it, and I didn't do it, and I didn't do it? No. He was subjected to all of the cross-examination that the State wanted to subject him to.

And the only thing he could say on direct and cross is that he didn't do it, and that he wasn't there, and that he didn't rob her, and that he didn't break into her apartment.

The evidence overwhelmingly supports the conclusion, at least by appearance, that his appearance is not that of the intruder in her home, and not that which was given to you by all the witnesses that testified in this case.

Just a brief more about the identification process. Of the individuals that you heard testify, I would suggest that you ought to think about those that were not in a position of an excited state when they saw whoever it was that they were looking at on that day.

I think we can agree and the evidence overwhelmingly supports that Z and her daughter were in an excited state. The State says that the conditions were bright, and the lighting is good inside the apartment. I don't want to characterize the evidence on that, but my belief is that there is no evidence in the record as to the lighting conditions in the apartment.

I think there is a photograph of a lamp, but there is no evidence as to what the lighting conditions were at the time. Let's just assume that it is ideal. But I don't think that there is any evidence to support lighting conditions in the apartment.

She is bleeding, and I don't think there is any mistake about that. Any human being would be more concerned about that situation than anything else. But on the evening of June 3rd, what does she tell the police? Whether she told them everything or not is—well, you have to be the judge of that, but she told the police that she told the individual that she was not going to look at him so that she could not make an identification.

And she admitted when I read to her from her own statement that she told the police that I didn't look directly at him. That I didn't look directly at him. Those are the words that she gave to the police on the evening of June 3rd.

Michele Purtrallo was in a good position to see, and talking to her friend, and she is a little off in her times, but she shouldn't be downplayed for that. We all know that it doesn't take four minutes to run from one end of the building to the next as shown in the photographs.

And whether it is 40 seconds or 60 seconds, or whatever, what is a reasonable period of time that she would have had to see the person that she saw at the time? And that the two individuals that were together, and that were aroused about a person's appearance; that is, aroused as citizens by the person's appearance, were Mr. Phucas and Mr. Schwartz.

Why? Because George saw the individual outside of his apartment at 3:30 when he got home. That was his testimony, and he was up in his apartment, and he looked out the window, and he saw the person. And he saw him a second time when he was up and about.

And Mr. Schwartz was understandably suspect or suspicious about this person, because he had seen him four times that day, four times under circumstances that we would all like to have seen an individual at that time; a bright, clear day, rested, no medications, no prescriptions, no alcohol, just running some errands and conducting his normal daily affairs, and coming out the door and looking down the sidewalk is a clear opportunity to see the person under circumstances that are not presented with excitement, and a reasonable opportunity to see everything that is there to be seen, and to reflect the description of the person as being oriental.

And why oriental? Because a new oriental family had recently moved into the development, and he did not consider it at the time to be suspect. He got into his car, and drove off towards the drug store, and looked back and saw the person sitting near the area of his front steps.

There was nothing exciting about that situation that would interfere with his objective ability to see what was there to be seen. The next opportunity is when he is in his apartment using the phone, and looking out that large glass window that is depicted in the photographs, and again moving in a direction from left to right, he sees the same individual; an oriental, with dark black hair, sunglasses. And later on in the day up around the basketball court, and in the area that is depicted in Defendant's Exhibit Number 75, he again sees the individual, the same person, with George, the same individual that Mr. Schwartz saw earlier in the day. He noticed him. He noticed him and the individual was at the picnic tables moving in the direction of 423.

He saw the person and was looking at him, and it was the same person; with a bag, oriental appearance, dark hair. He saw the person 10 minutes later run up a hill in the area of the basketball court. He got as close as the distance between Mr. Lee and Mr. Schwartz as depicted in State's Exhibit Number 17.

It is the same person, and the same weather conditions, and no obstructions, and ample opportunity to see, and he tells George to follow him to the car, and when the person got down there, to go down there and get that tag number. That's what he told him. That is what we expect of all of our citizens under ideal circumstances.

And that is to be observant, to be watchful, to be attentive, and to take note. And it is not a situation where you would be suspect about somebody like Mr. Schwartz. He is not telling us at the last minute, and on the eve of the trial, and giving us this information to somebody for the first time.

He was interviewed by the police on June 3rd, 1980, and gave the exact same information. And you saw him, and if you took notice the way that I noticed, you saw the manner in which I brought X up, and the manner in which Mr. Schwartz confronted him and answered the question if he was the person that you saw on those occasions on June 3rd, 1980, and he said no. He said no.

There are many points, many issues that will be discussed at times in the future about the vagueness of eyewitness identification, but I think you have enough to handle at this point in time. The State does have the burden of proving beyond a reasonable doubt the guilt of any accused that stands trial in the courts of this country, or any court in the State.

The Defendant is presumed to be innocent. He has plead not guilty, and he has protested the situation. He has protested his innocence, and he has taken the stand under oath and denied it. And the overwhelming evidence supports that denial, and I would respectfully suggest that the evidence supports a reasonable and a fair, and a unanimous conclusion on your part that he should be found not guilty. Thank you."

During Davis's dissertation, Anne Harrington was quietly taking notes. She was studying Davis's remarks with great intensity and she was determined to win this case.

As she had said to me, initially, when I had first met with her, "It is very unusual for a prosecutor to lose a case...we analyze the evidence very carefully, and when we're sure; *really* sure, well, then we go to trial."

So she went back up to the Judge and then faced the jury with her rebuttal closing arguments:

"Thank you, Your Honor. To what I am sure will be your intense personal relief, you can see that I don't have as nearly as many notes this time as I did when I stood up before you last time.

I would like to take an opportunity to make a few comments directed in rebuttal to some of the arguments that Mr. Davis made so eloquently to you just a few minutes before. You have heard during the course of the trial references being made to the attorneys as being officers of the court, and of course that is always true.

But I don't think it has escaped your watchful eye that the attorneys in the case are advocates, and it is their function to argue their side of the case, and it is Mr. Davis' function and his responsibility, and his solemn duty, to represent his client to the absolute best of his ability.

So, it does not come as a surprise to me, and I hope that it doesn't to you, that in his arguments to you that he mentioned, of course, the bits and pieces of the evidence that are favorable to his client.

And certainly in doing so he makes a very impressive presentation as an advocate, and very eloquent, and very well-reasoned and well-argued. And I would ask you certainly to look around the aspect of the advocate, and not to lose sight of all of the other things that you know that were never mentioned by Mr. Davis in his argument.

And specifically the two categories that I want to mention to you, and which will surely spring to your mind, and that you will recollect from your own notes, are the portions of the testimony in which in the interest of his client that he did not mention in his argument.

A great deal has been said about the oriental man described. It was an oriental man. Well, I'm sure that you will recall that almost all of these witnesses stood up and said that he has an oriental, Polynesian, kind of, type of appearance.

And words to that effect, and I am not exactly sure, but perhaps a half-breed, or perhaps this. Not just oriental. Oriental was not isolated out. Mr. Davis was fond of taking the police notes up to each witness and confronting them with them, and saying didn't you say that to the police?

In each and every case, we tried to establish that those were the notes of the police officer, and not the written statement of the person who made the observations. They told you from the witness stand what their recollections were, regardless of what the police wrote down on June 3rd.

And that is why I asked you to keep sight of what was actually going on. Interviews were being conducted as rapidly as they could, and notes being taken. And the first and foremost responsibility of the police on June 3rd is to find the person responsible for the attack, and not preserve testimony to be used in court two years down the road.

The best testimony is what the witnesses say and what they recollect, and you have their descriptions firsthand. You wrote them down on your pads, and I suggest that you look at them carefully, and you will see that the description that they gave you was X, and it matches the way that he appears.

My next point is that there are a couple of pieces of evidence that cause Mr. Davis and his client a great deal of difficulty, particularly Z and Mr. Ward. So, it is a very effective technique for an attorney to perform some sort of character assassination on those people.

And I think what Mr. Davis was attempting to do was to paint Z as a hysterical neurotic before you; and also Mr. Ward as an incorrigible, degenerate, perjuring liar, so that you will absolutely disregard anything and everything that they have to say.

And I would submit to you that that is not fair, and that is not what you saw from the people who testified and took the stand. The fact that Z has some attorneys representing her is no more relevant to the merits to this case than the fact that X has two sitting by him, and has had every single day during this trial.

It is not relevant, and it is offered as a red herring, and it is not worthy of consideration, and you should ignore it. If you determine that Mr. Ward is such a horrible person who would do this kind of thing, then that is the consideration that you make.

And you saw the man on the stand, and you heard him offer his apologies. You heard him say that I didn't want to get involved. And perhaps at the time you even related it to the way you felt when you were selected to sit on this jury. God, it couldn't have come at a worse time, and this is so inconvenient. But it is my civic duty, and I am going to do it.

That is what Mr. Ward is talking about, and not that he is a liar, a perjurer, a degenerative human being. I think it is fair for you to judge people on what you saw and what you heard, and not certainly on the argument of the advocates, the attorneys who want you to believe any particular set of facts.

Mr. Davis would like you to accept some of the witnesses testimony, but he would also like you to ignore some of the others, and I would argue to you that he can't have it both ways. And what I am specifically referring to is that he said that he wants you to accept everything that Mr. Schwartz and Mr. Phucas say, because that is favorable.

But he also wants you to accept everything that Mr. Kornhouser said. Well, Mr. Kornhouser, and Mr. Phucas, and Mr. Schwartz, say different things. Now, we are sure that they are talking about the same person, but once again use your human experience, and the result of your collective lives.

Two of them say a Plymouth Arrow, and one says a Pontiac Sunbird, and one offers the tag number to the police that he isn't even sure is correct, because he said that he didn't get that good of a look at it. He gave the letters that he thought it was. But he wasn't sure if it was what he saw.

And he sent the police on what turned out to be a wild goose chase to try and track down this car with this tag number that the officers told you that they could not connect to anyone who in any fashion resembled someone who might have been involved in this case.

The police cannot create the suspect. They can only go on what the people tell them, and when the people give them conflicting information, the police are not lazy or incompetent simply because they can't miraculously find the person from information that may not be correct.

You saw the detectives, and you heard all of the measures that they took to try and locate a Pontiac Sunbird. We have heard differing descriptions. It is as plausible that they are all incorrect about the make of the car as Mr. Kornhouser was right, and we can't say accept everybody's testimony, because it is all different.

That is your responsibility, and that is why you are asked to sit through the testimony, sort it out, and make a determination as to what actually happened.

Now, Mr. Davis in his remarks asked you to consider the kind of person that his client is. There is no evidence for you to consider as to the kind of person that his client is. We heard from the members of his family, and we heard from many of his friends.

And I would submit to you that if you search through your pads that you will not hear any reference to the kind of person that he is. So, once again, this is a remark that is not based on any evidence, and designed to appeal to your pity, or your passion, or your sympathy. Your oath is that you can't consider that, and you should ignore that.

Now, there are a couple of valid points that I want to address that Mr. Davis made, particularly Mr. Schwartz's testimony. I will not stand in front of you and tell you that Mr. Schwartz committed perjury, or that he wasn't telling the truth.

He was doing what everyone else did in this case, describing for you to the best of their ability what they saw and what they remembered. But I submit that when you compare Mr. Schwartz's testimony with all of the other people that you will see one thing.

You will see that he saw a man three times earlier on that day, wearing a yellow shirt, an oriental man, that he immediately associated with the family that had moved into the building where he lived.

The fourth time, he sees the subject carrying a bag. He is with George Phucas, and we are all talking about the same man. How does he see that person? He sees him running towards him for a little bit, and then he sees him from the back of the head.

All of the other descriptions have the description of a blue shirt, a blue striped shirt, and Mr. Schwartz says a yellow shirt, and based on that I would submit to you that the person he saw earlier in the day is not the same person he saw later in the day.

And I would offer you one further piece of evidence that I think that you can support that with. Michele Purtrallo and Robert Kornhouser; Michele Purtrallo actually selected X's photo from the array, and said that this is very similar looking to the man.

Robert Kornhouser said that I know X, and I can't say if he is the guy or not. He is similar looking from build and appearance. Well, Mr. Schwartz couldn't even go that far.

So, I think you can look to those pieces of evidence, and compare them to the rest of the witnesses, and you will satisfy yourself that Mr. Schwartz saw a man, and there is no doubt in his mind, and had confused him with the man that he later saw running with a bag.

So, I thought it was very important to establish when he saw the bag, and he said it was only on the fourth time when he viewed him that day to the best of his recollection.

As to the mustache, we have heard a lot of testimony from X's relatives, and from his friends, and you have got a lot of photographs. I would submit to you that facial hair and beards can come and go, and they are easy to fake. The testimony that you have to depend on is the testimony of the woman who was in the best position to have a good look at this person in making her identification.

And that is Z. If that is all that you had to depend on, I would say that Mr. Davis' point is very well taken. That's real risky. Maybe she did see him at Sir Walter Raleigh Inn, and that face fixated in her mind. And that is what she is basing it on. But it can't explain away Mr. Ward.

Mr. Ward did not have lunch at the Sir Walter Raleigh Inn, and Mr. Ward said X is the man that I saw on June 3rd, 1980. When you consider all of the testimony in the case, putting aside vagaries of eyewitness identification: you have heard it a lot, and you will hear it again.

So, I would urge you to not only look at the eyewitness identification, but also the circumstantial evidence in the case, and the connection with the place, and the familiarity with the layout of the development, and the proximity of the work, access to a yellow car, similarity of the tag number, and then look at the time card that relates to June 3rd, 1980.

And you will see that there is an altered time card, and there is no punch out time, and that time card was not corrected until Saturday. After you have considered all of the evidence, I would ask you to return appropriate verdicts of ***guilty*** as to all counts."

XII. THE VERDICT

And so the trial came to an end. I was relieved and recalcitrant—I stubbornly refused to submit to Davis's description of me: he suggested that I was somewhat malfeasant by being surrounded by lawyers who purportedly were preparing to file a civil suit in the absence of a guilty verdict; and that I was testifying pseudo-hysterically by disguising myself in a hat and sunglasses so that X couldn't really see who I was.

Outside in the parking lot, Tom Faye came over to me. "I have some important information for you, do you have a few minutes? Can we go somewhere for coffee?" I was curious about what he had. Was there going to be a mistrial? Had I missed something? It was about 3:00 in the afternoon...still early. "Do you mind if my friend, Jim, comes along?" "No, of course not." Tom told us to follow his car—to a coffee shop nearby.

Once we got seated inside, I got right to the point. "So what's going on?" "Let's order some coffee first...Jim you want coffee?" Jim smiled his Irish smile and with some sparkle in his eye he said that he'd have his with a shot of whiskey in it. Tom laughed. "They don't serve booze here, Jim."

I was still wound-up from the closing arguments and anxious for closure, for the verdict, so I wanted to hear what Tom had on his mind.

"I've been doing some research into X's background. Anne did some but couldn't find anything that she could use. I guess my research was more clandestine than hers because I did find out something. But I found it too late. We could have used it if I had discovered it earlier but I only got the fax yesterday—and it's a real doozy; turns out that X was adopted." "What?" I gasped. Then I realized that's why he looked so different from his parents.

"Yep...adopted. It was real secretive. They tried to lose the paperwork. I doubt that the guy even knows that he was adopted. It's really very peculiar. He was adopted in Pennsylvania when he was still a baby. They were living where they are now and had three kids, so it's odd that they adopted him. So this changes the identification thing—where the witnesses—and you, too, were saying things like he looked like a half-breed, maybe Oriental or Hawaiian. So this changes everything, like if his real parents were criminals or one was Chinese or something..."

"But, Tom—you said it's too late—the trial's over and we're waiting for the verdict, how can this change *anything*?" I asked.

"Look, I don't want to say this, but if the verdict is "not guilty", we've got to file a civil suit against him...we'd have a much better chance of winning then."

"Are you suggesting that I go through this whole thing again?"

"Yes, I am. You see, he was under the age of 21 when he committed the crime, so his parents are going to be liable. *They've* got money. His father has a top job at IBM and the place they own, their house, well it's worth about a half a million dollars...that's why Davis was so concerned about your lawyers he knows what your option is. You know, he's still an idiot because he talked about all of your lawyers without knowing that I'm the only one involved in the case. You've got Elliott, and he's just a friend that you consult with, and Quinn was looking into Y's beating on the playground and Davis got that all screwed-up."

Jim was digesting all of this. "You know, Z, he has a very good point. I can't believe it—the bastard was adopted. It's too bad Anne didn't know about that."

"No." I looked into my coffee cup. "No, I can't go through this again. I just can't do it. I can't live like this anymore. Even if he gets off,

I can't fight him any more. I mean, what if he wins a second time? Then he'll come after me and kill me *next* time."

Tom, of course, was going to push this on me, so I finally said, "I'll think about it."

I thought to myself, "Are you done with me, yet, God? When will this ever end?"

Jim and me drove home in silence. Anne said that she expected a verdict the next day and suggested that we return in the morning.

So, the next day we drove that 70 mile drive back to the court.

I had given Tom's proposal a great deal of thought and made a decision that I would not file a civil suit if he was found "not guilty" and of course I was hoping for the best.

We arrived at the court house at around 9 a.m., just like we had for two arduous weeks, and it would finally be our last time in that grim building. The jury was still out so I spoke with Tom for awhile and let him know of my decision. He was disappointed, of course, but I was confident that we had won the case. In a way I felt heady like a dirigible that was losing its helium...I was cock-sure that the jury would find him guilty of all charges.

It was like hell waiting for them to return. I wanted to go outside and have a smoke but I was afraid that I would miss the sentencing. And then, around 10 a.m., the jury entered the court room.

"All rise!"

The Clerk stepped forward, and as he must have said a hundred times before: "Ladies and gentlemen, have you agreed upon your verdict?"

"We have, Your Honor."

And the verdict crashed into my ears like a bug that splats on your windshield in the middle of the summer.

"Please stand, Mr. Foreman, and the Defendant, X. Ladies and Gentlemen of the Jury, look upon the Defendant. What say you? Is he guilty or not guilty as to Count Number One, Assault with intent to murder?"

NOT GUILTY.

"As to Count Number Two, Assault with intent to maim?"

NOT GUILTY.

"As to Count Number Three, Robbery with a deadly weapon?"

NOT GUILTY.

"As to Count Number Four, Daytime housebreaking?"

NOT GUILTY.

I sat there in disbelief. Jim grabbed my arm and quickly led me out of the court room. Neither of us said a word. I was stunned. How could this guy just walk away? How could this happen?

Outside of the Courthouse, Detective Williams came up to me and said "Look I'm sorry, I'm *really* sorry, but we're going to arrest him right now. I've got a warrant. There's another lady he attacked and we've got a positive I.D...We'll get him this time..."

I just walked away. I didn't even say goodbye.

He got off.

And I continue to remain anonymous. I have been absorbed into society; a nameless victim of an atrocious crime.

I am Z.

ABOUT CRIME

Z is a victim of crime. There is no past-tense for this affliction. In the United States, 1 out of every 3 persons is a crime victim. This is an alarming rate for a society that is as productive and civilized as we are.

Many states now have agencies that provide counseling and victim's compensation for our brutalized citizens. But it is not enough. While our courts are overrun with criminal cases, our jails crammed with perpetrators, and "America's Most Wanted" is aired on television, we are being bombarded with Internet crimes.

Many organizations, both private and federal, are clearly trying to control and overcome the escalating crime rate in this country, but until our statistics say 1 out every 1,000 persons is a crime victim ... teach your children to be aware of their surroundings.